Reiki Rays

REIKI
from A to Z

Angie Webster

Copyright

Reiki is not a replacement for medical assistance. Always seek professional medical support if you experience anything that requires it. Seek the services of a competent professional if expert assistance is required.

To fully understand and to be able to apply the techniques described in this book, the reader should already be introduced to the healing magic of Reiki.

Table of Contents

Chapter 1 – Reiki Explained

How Intention Works

Intention is very important in energy healing, and in life. Everything we do starts with the vibrational energy of intention. From that intention come the thoughts, words and actions that become our life. These thoughts, words and actions draw the situations and people into our life that we encounter. It is all connected, and it all starts with intention.

The intention that we set is the vibrational state that we are operating from. It sets the tone for how we will behave, how our lives will be, and even how we will feel. It becomes who we are and how others perceive us. It is the "vibe" or energy we radiate. So even before we have thought, said or done anything, our intention for how we want to be in the world and the effect we want to have on the Earth is important. It is important to our healing work, as it sets the tone for what sort of energy we are putting into our work.

There is a frequent misconception about intention, however. When you set an intention, it is not the same as making a wish and waiting for the wish to be granted. When you set an intention you are acknowledging the flow from that intention, through you and into the world. You acknowledge that you are setting your energy to a state where your thoughts, words and actions will now begin to shift and follow through to the fulfillment of that intention, even if you don't know how that will happen.

Often we don't know how the end result of our intention will come to be. It may seem so big or so far away from where we are now that we can't imagine it clearly, or don't know the steps to get there. By setting the intention, we set the course for our energy to begin to shift in the ways it needs to for the intention to come to be, to the extent that we are ready and open to it. This brings change to our minds, hearts and lives. It changes our energy.

There is always change when you set an intention. We all set intentions every day, though we aren't always aware of them. Consciously setting an intention is different. It is a way of accepting responsibility for your life and for the power you have over it. If you set intentions for something to come to you or for a change to happen in your life, but you are unwilling to do or change anything in yourself or your life to allow that to happen, then you are blocking the intentions you set.

Both allowing and action are important to creative change. The only one in charge of your energy and your life is you. By being open to allowing change and to taking action to bring your intentions into being, you take full responsibility and control of your life. That can be a little frightening at first, but it is a great feeling when you step into it.

To use intention to expand your heart and your awareness, especially in service to others is a wonderful thing, and will serve you in the end. This is very much what we do when we set an intention for healing at the beginning of a healing session. We intend to be present for the client in a loving way, with an open heart, and allow healing energy to flow through. The intention is that the session be for their greatest and highest good, though we don't know what that may be or what the outcome will look like. We don't know the path the healing will take, either in the short term or in the long term. In order for the healing to be most effective, both the healer and the client must be open to change, expansion and possible action.

Having a clear understanding about intention can lead to more ease in reaching your goals and less frustration. Be open to the path that may arise for you when you set an intention and be prepared to walk it. Pay attention to the signs, even if they are unexpected. Listen to the energy within your own body and heart. Take the steps and opportunities that your mind opens to. Most of all, allow your heart and mind to open. That's what setting an intention is all about—changing the energy of your heart and mind.

How Do I Know if I Am Doing Reiki Correctly?

By far the most frequently asked questions I receive have to do with people who are not confident in their ability to practice Reiki, sometimes even on themselves. There are people who are afraid for a great many reasons, like fear of harming another by practicing Reiki, fear of placing their hands in the wrong positions, not being able to feel Reiki flowing or not having intuitive insights. Unfortunately, many times, these fears lead to the person not practicing Reiki, or to restrict their practice.

There is no wrong way to do Reiki, because you are not truly doing Reiki. It is more that you are opening to allow Reiki to go where it needs to, through you. You are offering to be a clear passageway by simply being willing. Reiki energy flows from the Divine Life Force, the same life force that supports all life. There is no wrong way for it to flow through you. It is intelligent energy. This energy flows naturally wherever it is needed, as long as it is not restricted. By receiving an attunement, you are inviting the Reiki energy to clear out any restrictions you may have that impede its natural flow into and through you. Once you are attuned, Reiki will simply flow when and where it is needed. You only need to place your hands on yourself or someone else for it to be fully received. **It really is that simple.**

Our logical minds want many steps to each process. Sometimes we want to see how something works by understanding each step and what function it performs. But since Reiki simply flows where it is needed, there aren't a lot of steps for us to remember. We can place one or both hands on or above the body and then simply allow Reiki to do what it needs to do. This is why remembering all of the hand positions or a particular order to do them in is not very important. The most important thing is that you continue practicing Reiki. Over time, this practice will help you recognize where to place your hands, in what order and how long to leave them there. You may feel most comfortable using specific hand placements, particularly in the beginning while you are learning to trust the Reiki and your intuition to guide you. But if you forget some of these, recognize that they are more to help you feel comfortable than to make Reiki work properly.

Because Reiki is an intelligent energy that supports life, it will not do damage to life. There are times when Reiki can feel very intense or uncomfortable as it heals an area very quickly or removes an energy blockage. If this discomfort becomes too much or the energy feels too overwhelming at any time, by you or a client, then simply stop and the discomfort will leave. This discomfort is not from harm or damage, but from strong healing or energy balancing. It will stop the moment you remove your hands. Never force a person to receive Reiki if they don't want it or if they ask you to stop, no matter what their reason is. While the Reiki won't cause damage, it is harmful to do something to a person when they don't want you to.

While many people feel tingling or warmth in their hands after they receive their first attunement and most times they channel Reiki, there are also many who don't. Some feel nothing at all in their hands the majority of the times they perform a Reiki treatment. Others feel it when they are first attuned but then the sensation goes away as they adjust to it. Everyone's experience with Reiki and with the attunements is completely unique and very special, no matter what they do or don't experience.

Continue to practice daily self-Reiki, even after the 21 day clearing process. Make it a goal to create a habit of doing at least 10 minutes of self-Reiki every day, no matter what. Make it just as important as bathing, eating and sleeping. It is ideal if you make the space in your day to set aside this time to devote just to Reiki practice. However, remember you can also do self-Reiki as you read, watch TV or a movie or any time you can place one or both hands on yourself. Your understanding of Reiki will grow as you continue to practice each day and your connection to it will increase. In this process, you will come to notice you are recognizing ways your intuition expresses itself, more and more. Your own healing will continue, as well. It may seem as if it is going far too slowly in the beginning, but remember—you are unique and special. **Every one of us has our own pace for healing and growth and our own way of experiencing the world. There is nothing wrong with you or with the way Reiki flows through you.**

If you still feel uncomfortable and would like personal reassurance, consult your Reiki Master. He or she may be able to help you feel better or answer your questions. If it has been a long time since you practiced Reiki and you feel as if you want to brush up on your knowledge, some Reiki Masters are now offering a Reiki Refresher course to help you do just that. These usually come with a booster attunement to help boost your confidence and refine the flow of Reiki energy.

Explaining Reiki to Others

One of the most interesting challenges I have met as a Reiki practitioner has been learning how to explain what Reiki is and the ways it works to help us to those who know little or nothing about Reiki. I find that a different explanation is needed depending upon the person to whom you are speaking.

Some people are ready to learn more than others, so it is best to tailor the explanation to the needs of the specific person. Many people will want to learn more as they take in a small amount of information, whereas if you overload them with too much information at once, they may lose interest or misunderstand something. Think of when you are explaining something very new to a child who has never heard of it before. It is best to give a small bit of information and let them lead the way with their questions.

reikirays.com

It may be easiest for you to think back to your own level of understanding when you first heard of Reiki. What sort of things did you wonder about? What information did you find confusing? What information did you find helpful? When I first the word Reiki years ago, I was very confused about how to pronounce it (RAY-key) and what it did. I decided it wasn't for me based on a few pieces of unclear information. This can be the case for many people, so go slow and easy. It is not going to be helpful information if you overwhelm the person and they may become confused.

The best way I have found to explain Reiki is to say that it is an energy healing method that is usually done by placing the hands in a series of positions over or slightly above the body. If the person wants to know more, I will explain that Reiki promotes healing by activating the relaxation response and helping the body to balance itself from a very deep level. Sometimes it is best to offer a demonstration of Reiki, if the person is open to that. The experience of Reiki says more than words ever could.

Something that can frighten people who are new to learning about Reiki is the use of spiritual terminology. This kind of terminology can lead to the fear that Reiki is a religious practice or that it goes against certain religions. It can also lead to thoughts that Reiki is ineffective. Many people are uncomfortable with the word "spiritual" or "spirit". Use your best judgment in deciding if the person is able to understand that healing occurs on all levels, including the soul or spirit level.

Some people will want you to explain how Reiki works. No one really knows the answer to this. But you can tell them that Reiki allows positive energy to flow into the body through the hands of the practitioner and that this balances and heals the energy in the body. You could also explain some of the things that Reiki has been scientifically shown to do, such as decrease pain levels, speed healing and relax the mind and body. Make sure that the person understands that Reiki can only do good and can never cause harm.

Let your own understanding of the person you are speaking to guide you in what to say. When a person wants to know more and is enthusiastic, you will sense that. Likewise, you will learn to sense when a person is not able to take in too much information. Remember, it is not your role to force information onto someone who is not ready to receive it. Allow time and patience and be at peace. When the person is ready to receive more information about Reiki, they will know it is time. As healers, part of the process is allowing things to go forward at the pace that is comfortable to each individual. And acceptance that each of our paths is different.

Explaining Distant Reiki

I have written about Explaining Reiki to Others, but I find that when someone who doesn't know about Reiki wants to know about distant Reiki, it becomes more difficult. Particularly if they want an explanation for how it works. Many people are somewhat able to understand the basic concepts of Reiki in general, but the thought that this could work for someone on the other side of the world can seem too much to take in.

My experience has been that those who are unfamiliar with energy in healing will ask if distant Reiki works through computers, via the internet or over the phone. They have a hard time understanding how a treatment can be sent without connecting it to something tangible for it to flow through that connects both parties.

I admit I was very skeptical of healing energy being real over long distances until I had had several experiences with it. My first experience was almost 6 years ago. A woman I was friends with was part of a group that met once a week to send healing energies to those in need. She offered to add my name to the list to help me with numerous health problems I had struggled with for years. I said yes, more to humor her than anything. I felt it couldn't hurt because I didn't think it was real.

I was surprised that I could actually feel the energy flow from this group of people each week on the night they met. Even when I forgot about the healing, I would realize I felt peace wash over me and my pain would ease. Within a short time, my health issues began to fade away. I also had more clarity of thought and ability to cope with life.

Yet, even when I learned about Reiki and energy healing, I was still skeptical that it could work. I had seen prayer work from long distances. I believed there also might be special people that could heal from far away. I doubted that anyone could be taught to do it. And I still doubted anyone who said they could do energy work from a distance until they proved it to me.

The telephone, cable TV and internet all use energy frequencies we can't see in order to function. The electricity in our homes does the same, as does a radio. All of these have to be tuned to the particular frequency they operate at in order to work. They all have ways to adjust the flow of energy built in so that we can turn them on, off or use them in a different way. And all of them were thought too unbelievable to be true when people first heard of them.

Distant Reiki works the same way. It is energy that must be "tuned" to the person it is being sent to. Once it is "tuned in"

What are Attunements All About?

One of the strangest and mysterious things about Reiki to those first investigating it is the attunement process. Even the word *"attunement"* leaves a bit of mystery. It sounds like a vague and unknown thing that is impossible to wrap the mind around because there is nothing in the experience to compare it to. This can even make it seem a little scary to some. So let's explore the attunement and bring some understanding to what it is, what it does, how it feels and what happens afterward.

An attunement is a part of the Reiki training process. It is something that only a Reiki Master is trained to do. The process can be seen as accomplishing two things. One is to do a very intense healing on the recipient, which goes very deeply into the energy channels, opening and clearing them.

This makes way for rapid healing to begin for the newly attuned Reiki practitioner. Opening and clearing these energy channels not only allows for a greater healing, it allows for the Reiki energy to flow more freely through them, so that the recipient of the attunement will now freely receive Reiki at all times, particularly when intending to receive it, and will also allow Reiki to transmit through them, flowing more easily through these energy channels.

We all have Universal Energy flowing through us and around us. It is everywhere, in fact. The Reiki attunement allows us to open up to this energy and become more aware of it than we normally are. It literally attunes us to it. When we come into the world as infants, we are much more in tune with this energy and as we become habitualized to this world, we lose the awareness of it. A Reiki attunement helps us to open our awareness to it.

Most people who have a Reiki attunement, even at the first level, can feel the energy flowing through their body, their hands, and sometimes their feet right away, sometimes even as the attunement is being done. This doesn't happen to everyone and a few only report minor sensations or none at all. They may not feel the energy flowing through them, but when they practice Reiki on another, they will be told that the energy is felt and shifts will be seen. In doing Reiki self-treatment after an attunement, even the newly attuned will feel peace, even if they don't feel a lot of heat or other sensations coming from their hands. The perception of the sensations is somewhat different for everyone and will vary from session to session, which is normal.

During the attunement, the Reiki Master will ask you to close your eyes and become still and prayerful or meditative, looking within yourself for the meaning and symbolism of the process to you. You may be asked to focus on your breath and to notice your center. The Master will then draw symbols which represent various healing energies, such as the power of love, harmony, the Unity of All or God with us, and one that helps to dissolve the illusion of time and space. These will be drawn in your aura and on your hands. There are some slight variations aside from this in the ways that different Masters do an attunement, so these are only the basics, not the entire process. Most Masters begin and end the process with a brief prayer or intention, which may or may not be spoken aloud.

People experience various different things during an attunement and your experience will be your own. Whatever you experience is exactly what is appropriate for you at the time. Don't get concerned about comparing with others or with what you read on the internet. Many people feel sensations of heat or tingling or of vibration rising up their spine or flowing down from the crown to the base of the spine or the feet. Some feel their hands grow hot. Many see colors or have visions. A few hear sounds such as music or bells or angelic voices. There are many possibilities. It is a rather profound and moving experience for many.

In the days after an attunement, many people have a healing response, often referred to as a healing crisis. This can last for up to two or three weeks, fluctuating in the symptoms and severity, and many teachers will teach that you should expect it to last 21 days. In truth, it varies from person to person and from one attunement to the next. Some people have no healing response at all, for some it is very mild, others are very sick for the first day or two with flu-like symptoms and then feel a lot better, with only mild emotional fluctuations for a week or two after that. For some, the healing response is almost entirely emotional, with emotions arising and releasing, maybe with crying spells or anger coming out and releasing. It may be gentle or not. It is best to simply observe and let the energies pass, journaling and processing as needed. Nearly everyone will notice that their life changes in some way after an attunement, even if it is only that their responses to things shift. Keeping a journal in the weeks after and attunement can help you track the process and is very interesting to look back on later, even if the changes seen mild or insignificant at the time.

Attunement Triggers Healing Crisis

Lots of people believe that once they are attuned to Reiki they will never be sick for very long again. They think they will be able to heal themselves from any illness they previously struggled with, no matter how long it went on. I thought this as well. The truth is, many people who are led to Reiki have a long history of being ill or of dealing with repeated loss or abuse in their life. I think perhaps some of them are guided to Reiki to help them learn to heal these patterns of illness and dysfunction.

But part of the learning process with Reiki is to learn that healing does not mean the same as cure. And healing rarely happens overnight and it almost never happens the way our logical minds plan for it. Healing is a messy process and it is not passive. Receiving Reiki is passive, but the healing itself is never passive. Inner work is done and shifts take place in the life of the person being healed. This is often a very uncomfortable process. And it can look and feel an awful lot like being very, very sick.

I often think of this the same way as I think of spring cleaning. You clean out a closet, a cabinet, a drawer or even a crowed, cluttered and messy room, filled with junk. When you do this, you have to pull all that junk out. It makes a huge mess all

Aside from a worsening of symptoms, some people feel very tired in the 12-48 hours after a Reiki treatment, or need to urinate or move their bowels more frequently. Some people notice they are much more emotional. Others may feel as if they are coming down with a cold or flu for several hours to a day. It is important that we advise those we treat to honor the needs of their body. If rest is what the body asks for, rest should be given. Their system is healing and this can be hard work, so it is a good idea to support the process. Extra water is highly recommended as well.

When a person feels badly, they may wonder if something is wrong. While unpleasant symptoms after receiving Reiki do not necessarily mean that there is a problem, it can happen that a new problem arises after the Reiki treatment. A person should always use their own internal guidance to make the best judgment for themselves regarding if a health care practitioner should be contacted.

Healers and Money

Is it wrong for healers and spiritual teachers to make a living helping others? Many struggle with this question. When we fall into the belief that we cannot use our talents to heal and make enough to live on, we limit how many we are able to offer healing to. We are, in a sense, rejecting our talent.

A living must be made in order for a healer or teacher to have shelter, food and clothing. If basic needs are not provided for, the healer suffers. The only option is to heal or teach less of the time so that a living may be earned another way. This means fewer are helped, healed and taught.

When healing work is done with a sense of service and gratitude, there is no need to feel that what we are doing is not important or should not be rewarded. We have all been

- Make you wealthy, make you win the lottery, etc. (though it can help heal underlying wounds with regard to money, such as feelings of greed or lack)
- Make anyone do anything (though it can bring about acceptance and trust in your own ability to make changes in your own life)
- Promise a cure of an illness (though it can bring balance to the underlying issue, ease pain and bring calm)

If a Reiki practitioner has promised you any of these things, or any specific outcome, please understand that you may not actually receive these results. Consider that you may be doing more harm to yourself by seeking the quick solution, the fastest relief to your problem. You may find that there is much more healing to be found by getting to the root of the problem, the underlying energies, and healing those. This may not offer you an end result you can foresee, and it won't be a quick fix in most cases, but it does offer long term healing and true healing. **Quick fixes never do and they often only prolong or worsen our suffering.**

It is definitely possible to move toward our own goals and desires using energy by making a choice and following through with actions. And often that will work. You don't even need anyone else to help you do that. **But if our ultimate goal is true healing, then it works even better to open**

ourselves to the larger energy and allow all of the channels of healing energy to be available to us. So many more options present themselves and underlying problems heal, sometimes so gently we aren't even aware of the process aside from the gradual changes. This truly helps relieve suffering and pain, both now and in the long run.

Is Reiki 'All in Your Head'?

In Western society, we are very protective of the scientific approach and insist that all things be looked at in an intensely logically manner. Science has greatly benefitted the world and is a wonderful tool. However, there is almost a fear of not seeing things through the filter of the hyper critical, extremely logical mind. This approach misses entire areas of the brain. It leaves out intuitive thinking, intention and emotion. In fact, it completely negates their importance in the scientific process, when these things likely play more of a role in the way the world functions than simple logic, facts and figures, more than things that can be directly seen, touched and easily measured. You may have heard the phrase 'not seeing the forest for the trees'. To me, this stiff approach is much like only seeing a single vein on a single leaf on a single tree and missing the entirety of the rest of the forest.

I often hear very scientific types say they are not satisfied with the evidence that has been shown in studies that Reiki is effective in helping in the care and treatment of illness, pain or immune function. There are a number of studies that show its effectiveness, and more are being completed all the time. However, very scientific people prefer studies that show a specific thing being effective in a specific way, preferably in a laboratory setting. This is not very testable with something like Reiki.

Reiki is done through intention, using the natural healing life force energy that is all around us and in us. Very little is scientifically known about how intention works or how it effects the outcome of studies, though what little is known has created some issues for researchers in other studies. It is difficult to examine the validity of the results of a study where the outcome is said to be determined by intention. How do you research intention? Or prove it? Do the researchers' intentions affect the outcome as well?

It is becoming fairly accepted by more and more in the medical community that Reiki does no harm and that it helps to relieve pain at the very least, and seems to balance the immune system and calm side effects of surgery and chemotherapy drugs in most cases as well. However, many lay people and scientific types as well still wonder if it is simply a placebo effect. And that is considered to be a negative, unscientific thing. Yet, I have always wondered, if it works and it's safe, what difference does it make what you call it?

I am asked quite often if Reiki is "all in people's heads". This question doesn't offend me at all. I know the mind is quite powerful. Intention is quite powerful. That isn't something to be defensive about. It is something to embrace fully! It makes no difference to me if someone wants to see Reiki as being "all in my head." That doesn't make it less real. Everything starts in your head, with an intention. And then it makes its way into reality. The people asking this question simply don't understand this yet. This is understandable because most people rarely do the things in their lives with purposeful intention. The intentions are there, but they aren't aware of them and don't choose them.

Reiki is a method of consciously and purposely aligning with kind and loving healing energies so that those energies may assist someone in finding their best possible version of themselves, body, mind and spirit. It relieves pain, it eases depression, it boosts the healing response. I think it would be really great if more "proofs" were seen, but truly, as long as it keeps helping people, I don't care if it's called a placebo. The healing is real, no matter where it is said to come from.

Empaths as Healers

Many of those who are drawn to the path of healing arts are also highly empathic. Being empathic has a range of meanings. They may be very aware of the needs and feelings of others and thus be very caring. Or they may actually feel the emotions of those around them, perhaps to the point that they have difficulty distinguishing when the emotions are their own or someone else's. Many empaths also feel the physical pains and illnesses of others. Again, many quite often have a difficult time separating another's symptoms from their own.

Empaths feel the world around them. It may be that this is why many are drawn to healing. They can feel where there is a need. This can be very useful in the healing arts. It can also cause difficulty. Seeing or feeling where targeted healing needs to be applied during a healing session is very helpful. Empath skills also help during scanning and clearing. Yet when an empath so deeply feels what they are trying to heal that they can't separate it from themselves, they begin to weaken themselves and block their own energy channels. It no longer helps their healing, it begins to hinder it.

Everyone wants to feel well. And all healers want to be effective and helpful at what they do. **Unfortunately, I think**

as empaths, we get the idea that we are meant to suffer along with those we help in order for our work to be effective. That somehow if we take on the suffering of our clients or even the suffering of the world, we will be helping. This is an error in thinking. **It is an error that limits us as healers and also makes us feel ill and leaves us carrying lots of physical and emotional pain.**

A big key to healing is to not resist what you are trying to heal and at the same time not pull it into yourself or absorb it. **When we can simply accept the issues our clients have from a place of non-judgement and love, we can let healing energy flow** freely. That shifts it. We don't need to take it on ourselves and suffer.

We also don't need to create resistance against whatever we are directing healing toward. When we see it as a problem that needs to be resisted, we create blocks in ourselves and we are also fighting what is a part of our client's reality in this moment. The most loving and healing thing to do is to love and accept where someone is—always. Whatever they are experiencing is a part of their path and will help them to reach the next part. **Your part in the path is to hold space as they walk their path, not to walk their path for them or to change their direction on the path.** Love, accept and send healing. Allow the process to unfold as it needs to. This leaves space for the client to find love and acceptance for themselves as well.

It can be challenging to learn to separate your own energy from that of others when you are a healer and an empath. It has certainly been my biggest challenge as a healer so far. It has been a practice more than anything. Learning to appreciate the path of others, heal my own inner wounds and feel less resistance to that which I see as a "problem" and simply let healing flow where it is needed has helped. **It can make for a very strong healer when you can make use of your empath skills without letting them overwhelm you.**

Demystifying the Symbols with Respect

The Reiki symbols are a subject of some fear and controversy. I recognized that I had avoided the subject of the symbols as much as possible and after some self-exploration I have realized that this was due to fear. I think whenever we are told that something is secret or hidden and must remain that way, it places a layer of concern over it. Maybe that isn't the original intent behind trying to shield the Reiki symbols, but it is possible that this contributes to much of the fear that many have around Reiki now.

When I began to be interested in energy medicine and started to seek out information about Reiki, I came across the information regarding the use of symbols. That seemed a little strange to me at the time, but I wasn't deterred until I heard that they were kept secret and were considered sacred. That triggered lots of fear in me back then. I had fear-filled images of secret societies or cults or strange, extreme religious organizations. No matter what I read that said Reiki isn't affiliated with a religion, it didn't help me feel better. I felt that would be what many cults would say! There are still lots of people out there who think like this and their blogs and websites are everywhere. They are very fearful of Reiki, the symbols and the attunements. These are the very true and real (though not accurate) fears they have.

My fear almost kept me from looking any further into Reiki. I knew I was meant to work with energy medicine, but I was not sure that Reiki was right for me if secret symbols were involved! Especially if I couldn't even see what they looked like or know what they meant. Fortunately, I was able to do a Google search and find many images of the symbols, explanations of their meanings and even videos about them. I soon felt relieved and continued forward on my Reiki path.

However, once I took my first Reiki class, I too was convinced that the symbols must remain guarded. I must admit that I never fully understood why, though I was again very fearful about it. It was as if I was afraid something very bad might happen if the symbols were to be shared. Which is strange since already knew they were readily available on the internet and in many books for whoever might like to see them. Yet I absorbed this fear from others in the Reiki community and began to wear it like a badge, even though I wasn't sure why. I vowed to understand it. Both the reason to protect the symbols and the fear of letting them be seen.

The Reiki symbols, like all symbols represent something larger. They are not simply something in and of themselves. They are energy which represents and carries the energy signature of a larger energy. The reason they hold that larger energy is because we agree that it does. We give it the intention to mean that and keep giving it that intention over and over. With time, the energy of the symbol grows stronger with the energy of the intention and it holds that. **If it were not for the intention, the symbol itself would mean very little because it would not hold enough energy.**

A symbol that has been infused with a lot of meaning will carry that meaning strongly. Any emotion the symbol has attracted to it will also be attached to it, such as the deep respect and sacred feeling the Reiki symbols carried for so long. The symbol of many religions, such as the Christian cross, are examples of symbols that carry deep respect and sacredness, as well.

The Reiki symbols are placeholders for the healing energy of the Divine and the different frequencies that can be brought through. They deserve very deep respect, not because of the symbols themselves, but because of what they represent and the deep meaning it can have to each person who works with the energy or experiences it on a healing level.

We don't need to pretend we are hiding the symbols or that we can't talk about them. They have not truly been hidden in some time. But we can do our best to discuss them and use them with the respect they deserve, without making the display of them something frivolous and commonplace. We can each look inside ourselves and ask what that means to us.

I feel it is important to discuss the symbols in an open but respectful manner so that fear energy is no longer a part of what is being infused into Reiki as it becomes more well-known and mainstream. It is my hope that energy healing will become widely used by all people and it would be a shame if either fear or disrespect of this wonderful tool were to hold that back.

Anger and Worry

The first two Reiki principles or precepts state, "Just for today, I will not worry" and "Just for today, I will not anger." I admit, when I got attuned to Reiki, I spent a lot of time pondering what these really meant. I even wondered if the true meaning was somehow distorted or lost slightly in the translation from Japanese to English. In truth, I still wonder a bit! These two principles are very important and they can guide our daily lives and even the other principles, but we need to be careful how we understand them.

I don't think it is intended that we pretend we don't ever feel the emotions anger or fear (which is what drives worry). Nor are we meant to stifle these emotions when they arise. The wording implies that we are not meant to feel or acknowledge these emotions, but that is not healthy. Most healers recognize that stuffing emotions creates illness.

Emotions are useful tools that give us information about ourselves, our bodies, our environments and our relationships. We would have a much more difficult time on our journey of healing and growth without our emotions as indicators. They can be uncomfortable or very pleasant, but either way, they are giving us useful information. It is up to us to decide what to do with it after that.

That is where the first two precepts come in. We can receive the information that we are feeling anger and then choose to react and then we are very involved in the anger. At that point, it might be correct to say we *are* angry, whereas before we simply *felt* angry. The other choice is to notice we are feeling anger and not to feed the thoughts, but to simply notice them and notice the feelings in our body. Not easy. Once we allow our thoughts and reactions to become involved in the anger, we are a bit lost in it until we either consciously decide to disengage from those or all the outside stimuli that are feeding it subside for awhile. It only takes about 20 minutes for anger chemicals to dissipate from the bloodstream after they are released, assuming we don't keep feeding them with new thoughts of anger.

Similar things are true for the emotion of fear. We notice that we are feeling fear and then we can choose to either become locked into thoughts of worry and 'what-if' thinking, creating anxiety in our mind and body, or we have the opportunity to choose to be open to seeing what happens if we face the fear, even if we have to do it in small steps. We can try being open to not knowing what will happen, if fear of the unknown is what is we are feeling. There is more opportunity and wonder in the mystery than in all the what-ifs our minds could ever create!

More than anything, the first two precepts are really about staying present and aware. You have to be aware of your emotions and your thoughts in order to make a conscious choice in how you will respond to any emotion or habitual thought process. When we live caught up in thoughts of anger, we are really thinking not about what is going on right now, but about what went on when we got angry and the ways we imagine it will make us angry in the future. When we are feeling fear, we are focused on the future and our ability to handle the present is diminished the longer we are caught in worry. You will always be better able to handle any situation when you are aware of the present.

Never feel like you have to ignore or suppress your emotions. Doing so traps toxins in your body and causes illness. Not only that, but tuning out your emotions also tunes out one of the best paths you have to spiritual growth and to hearing what your body and mind need to heal. Choose wisely how to tend to them, but never ignore these tools!

Chapter 2 – Self-Healing

The Importance of Self Reiki

The very first time we get attuned to our first level of Reiki, we are told that we need to begin doing Reiki self treatments daily. Daily life is often hectic and it can be easy to lose track of why it is so important to do self Reiki every day. However, it is of great benefit to us to make this a practice, for many reasons. We can even make it a practice to find unique and interesting ways to fit in a bit of Reiki as we go through our day, making our self practice our own.

Remember, even if you only have time for a little Reiki, it is still good. A little is better than none! And keep in mind that it needn't be a complex process. You can simply place even one free hand on yourself, on any part of your body, and ask Reiki to flow. No need focus or direct it. Reiki will flow where it is needed.

Reasons That Daily Self Reiki is Important

1.   During the 21-day healing cleanse after an attunement at any level, most practitioners experience some type of physical or emotional healing crisis. Doing daily self Reiki can ease the process and ease the transition.

2.   Doing self-Reiki allows you to become more and more aware of the Reiki energy and the many ways it works, as well as allowing you to understand better how Reiki works in and through you as a practitioner. Thus, it refines your attunement to the energy. You can't be an expert at something unless you work with it regularly and understand it on a very deep level!

3.   The more you allow Reiki to flow through you via self Reiki, the more healing you will allow Reiki to bring to you. Even if you only came to the Reiki path to heal others, you must be aware that healing others begins with healing yourself.

4.   The longer you do self Reiki on a regular basis, the more you learn about yourself and your personal growth will expand. You begin to understand yourself in new ways, physically, emotionally, mentally, and spiritually. This begins to apply to others and the world around you.

5.   You will be more focused and stress will have less of an effect on you. One of the biggest things Reiki can do for you is reduce your stress level.

Reiki works on a very subtle level. Because of this, there are many ways you will not even notice that Reiki is having an effect on your life at first, even if you are very aware of its presence and its power. Those subtle effects only make themselves apparent over time. It may soon feel as though problems are not as big as they once were or that the solutions simply come more easily. Sometimes the solutions may seem to come about ways that defy explanation. Finding the time for even a few minutes of Reiki here and there each day will make a huge difference in your life and in your understanding of Reiki.

Self Reiki

It is very important for Reiki practitioners to treat themselves frequently. Daily is best. When you give Reiki to yourself you are staying directly in touch with the sensation of offering and receiving Reiki. For those that are new to Reiki, acquainting yourself with these sensations is helpful. Self Reiki is an excellent way to learn what these sensations are like as well as to experience healing through Reiki, firsthand. When you heal yourself, you become a better healer for others.

Self Reiki will work for you in the same way that receiving Reiki from someone else does. It heals on the mental, spiritual, emotional and physical levels. Anything that manifests on a physical level will have a deeper root in the emotional, mental or spiritual realm. Regular self Reiki treatments can ease these deeper imbalances before they manifest on the physical level. Aside from keeping your physical body well, this allows for greater emotional freedom, decreased mental stress and deeper spiritual growth. It will also improve your ability to spot an imbalance early, prior to it manifesting physically.

Giving Reiki to yourself can seem different than when giving Reiki to others. This sometimes leads to the nagging feeling that Reiki is not flowing or the self treatment is being done wrong. However, there is no need to be concerned. Reiki always flows where it is needed, including when you are treating yourself. Trust the Reiki. Worry during the treatment will only cause resistance and inhibit your ability to feel the flow of Reiki. Relax and enjoy the healing.

Just as when you are treating others, self treatment sessions will vary from one time to another. You may have times where you don't experience anything at all. Other times, you may be deeply moved and feel emotions coming up for release. You may feel warmth, cold or heaviness in your entire body or only in certain areas of the body. Sometimes you may feel the Reiki flowing intensely from your hands. You may also feel your body pulling the Reiki from your hands. Even if you don't feel the sensations, Reiki is coming through and going where you need it most at that time. Allow yourself to completely feel whatever you are experiencing; in the same compassionate way you would allow a patient to do so. Observe your breath and any sensations you feel as you relax deeply.

When you are feeling unwell, treat yourself with Reiki as soon as possible. Even a mini Reiki self treatment can help shorten the duration of the imbalance, or even eliminate it altogether. Practice developing an awareness of your emotional, mental and physical state. In this way, you will be better able to self treat early and stay well.

Self Reiki is a wonderful tool to use when you have injured yourself. Apply Reiki directly to the injured area for at least one minute; longer if your intuition guides you to do so. You may find that bleeding stops faster, cuts heal more quickly and swelling and bruising may be minimized when you apply Reiki to an injury. Self treating an injury right away is best, but even injuries that aren't treated until later will heal more quickly with Reiki self treatment.

Don't wait until you are sick or injured. Make daily self Reiki part of your routine. When you treat yourself daily, you will begin to notice that you feel better, and are more aware of the flow of energy in your body. Your health will improve and you will find that things seem to flow more easily, even on challenging days!

Self-Healing Reiki Meditation

In addition to doing daily self-Reiki, doing Reiki meditations can be a very useful practice. It can give our healing a boost, help us tune in more deeply with Reiki, learning how it moves through us and is working with our bodies and energy systems. I have come to have a fuller understanding of how the energy system works and how to work with it by doing regular Reiki self-healing meditations. It has greatly strengthened me, accelerating my healing process and it has also helped me use Reiki more effectively with others.

Reiki self-healing meditation can be done alone or in combination with a Reiki self-treatment. It is nice to use this when you are not able to do a full self-treatment, such as when you are in public. I have used this meditation when I was very ill and simply didn't feel up to lifting my arms to the upper hand positions. I can imagine it would be very beneficial to someone who had been in an accident and was incapacitated in some way. All the Reiki self-healing meditation requires is your mental focus and your imagination.

To do the meditation, close your eyes and begin to relax and settle your attention into your body and your inner world. Notice your breath for two to three cycles. Allow yourself to settle into the rhythmic flow as it moves in and out of your body. Next, see if you can notice the beating of your heart in the background as it pulses blood through your body. If you cannot hear or feel this, then simply imagine the pulsing flow of blood from your heart, coursing beautifully through all the vessels of your body, keeping you healthy and alive.

Begin to allow Reiki to flow naturally along these pathways of air and blood, carrying Reiki throughout your body as it goes. Infuse the symbols into the flow. Perhaps begin with the Power symbol to bless the process, but use whatever symbols feel appropriate to you. Each time you use this process, you will feel led to use different symbols in different areas and that's fine. Follow your own intuition. Take your time adding any symbols you feel are correct for you, or use none and simply send Reiki.

Next, turn your attention to the brain. Ask your brain to open, relax and release anything it needs to let go of at this time. Pause for a moment and allow this to take place. You may feel a coolness expand across the head or a lightness. Whatever you feel is OK. Allow the sensation and notice what it is. Imagine yourself as a very small being of light, standing in the center of your brain. Look around and notice what you see and feel. Do some areas feel or look lighter or denser? Do you have a sense that some areas would like to receive Reiki energy? Begin to direct Reiki to the areas that seem dense or that you feel led to give to. Again, infuse any symbols that you feel you are led to, wherever you feel they are appropriate.

When you are finished, turn to face the spine and ask it to open, relax and release anything that it needs to let go of at this time. You may feel a sense of opening, lightness or coolness flowing down the center of your spine. Have your small light being self begin to direct Reiki energy down the spinal column and into the back muscles, nerve tissue and all supporting structures. Once again, infuse any symbols that feel appropriate to you.

Take a moment to scan your body. Tune in to the energy pathways and the physical sensations. Do you notice any densities or areas or tightness? Pain? Perhaps you feel or sense areas of thickness or other uncomfortable energy. Take this opportunity to ask your small light being form to move to any area you notice these things in and begin directing Reiki energy. Make use of the symbols wherever you feel the need. Place your attention in any organs that are in need of attention and ask them to open, relax and release. Then direct Reiki energy to them for however long they need it.

Lastly, scan the aura and send Reiki to any areas that feel dense or weak. Place all the symbols in the aura to seal it. You may choose to place them wherever, and in as many places, as you feel is correct to you. This may change from one time to the next and you are encouraged you to follow your intuition. Consider areas such as above the head, below the feet, at each chakra (front and back) and at each side, yet if you are guided to place the symbols elsewhere, or to leave out one of these areas, please do that.

May this Self-Healing Reiki meditation lift you to your greatest and highest good.

Simplified Self Reiki

A lot of times people feel that doing self-Reiki takes too much time, or that it's too complicated. They worry that they aren't doing it right or that they aren't feeling what they are "supposed to" be feeling. My response to this is almost always some version of this— "Simplify, simplify, simplify!"

Reiki is one of the simplest things you will ever do. There is very little "doing" to it. It is mostly just allowing and being. However, that is difficult for our minds to accept. The mind likes to be active and working. It's fidgety. That's normal and OK. But it can become a little like a very young child that asks continuous questions and searches for something to do when what it really needs is to simply be still for a moment to drift off to sleep. We do this with Reiki. We search for ways to delay resting into its simplicity and stillness. We tell ourselves we don't have time, we have other things to do, we are doing it wrong, etc.

When I first began doing Reiki, I relished the new energy flowing through me. For at least 6 months prior to my training, I had been doing a morning treatment using deep breathing and most of the hand positions (see Appendix 1) used in self Reiki. I loved the way this felt and it really helped my mind and body! After training and attunement, instead of continuing this very simple practice with the new and lovely energy of Reiki, I abandoned it in favor of a long Reiki session each morning. I loved my long and deeply personal Reiki sessions and woke up early each day in order to have them. There were times, though when it felt as if something was off. Like I was making it more complicated than it needed to be, and by doing so, missing the bigger picture.

I have since explored that and decided to return to a more simplified version of daily self-Reiki practice. Maybe it will resonate with some of you, as well.

1.   Sit comfortably. You may like to sit on the floor, if that is comfortable for you, as this is very grounding. If it is difficult for you to sit on the floor comfortably, sit up straight on a chair or stool in a way that allows you to reach your lower back.

2.   Place your hands in each of the positions for self-treatment, as shown on the chart offered on Reiki Rays. **In each hand position, take three deep breaths**. See if you can notice these breaths moving into your lower belly, allowing your belly to be as soft and relaxed as possible.

3.   After three deep breaths, **move your hands to the next hand position. Continue until you have treated in all the hand positions.**

4.   That's it! Simple!

The entire treatment only takes about 10 minutes or less. There is never any question about what to focus on, since your attention is only on your breath going in and out of your low belly and counting to 3 breaths. You will notice that tension melts away and any pain decreases as you do the treatment. It is fairly immediate. Even if you can't feel any energy flowing through you, this shift is plenty to help you see that the treatment is working and helping you heal.

I am loving the return to this simplified version of Reiki self-treatment! I find that it is actually helping me more than the more complicated version.

Violet Flame Mirror Self Reiki

This is a bit of a quick tip that is a combination of a mediation technique I learned from a spiritual teacher years ago and the use of Reiki. It will quickly refresh you as you go through your day. You can also slip away into a bathroom in a stressful situation and use this technique and come away better able to be present, loving, and diplomatic. It is very calming and healing, and though it only takes a few minutes, it can actually serve to heal layers of issues.

The Violet Flame is a living energy that can assist you in healing and in releasing energies that are ready to move out of your system. It is wonderful at transmuting energy and at it will likely help you to begin to understand more about transmuting energy as well.

To use this technique, **stand in front of a mirror** and offer Reiki to yourself. You can do this by directing the flow from your hands, or by beaming Reiki from your eyes. Allow the focus of your eyes to settle on your Crown chakra and intend that Reiki flow there as you take 1-3 deep breaths. **Ask the Violet Flame to assist you and feel it flow with the Reiki in to your Crown. With every out breath, release anything that needs to move out of you now.**

Direct your attention to the Third Eye and repeat these same steps. **Do this with each chakra** until you have reached the Root chakra. Then direct the flow of Reiki and the Violet Flame toward the *hands* for a breath or two as well, asking that all you touch be blessed. You may also choose to do this with the *feet*, asking that your footsteps touch the Earth with peace and love.

Lastly, envision the **Violet Flame embracing your entire body.** Feel it encircling you and clearing away any remaining debris that may have been loosened. Allow yourself to let it go. Feel the Violet Flame moving through you and lifting you back into Divine grace and alignment. Feel the wave of peace the moves through you. Take a deep breath.

You may wish to do a version of this between healing sessions with clients to assist you in releasing any energy that you may have picked up from the session, as a form of **energy hygiene.** For this purpose, it might be good to focus especially on the head, heart and hands, as well as doing the full body clearing at the end.

After doing this very loving exercise, your chakras will be cleared and balanced and you will feel cleansed and very relaxed. Remember, Reiki reaches through time and space, so there are no bounds to the ways this may heal your life! Be open to what your experience may be.

Tip for Self-Reiki of the Spine

Do you treat your back with self-Reiki? There are wonderful reasons to treat the spine, back and kidneys when we do Reiki treatments, and especially when we do our daily self-Reiki. The spine is a major line of energy flow in our system. This flows from our brain all the way down into our pelvis. Most everyone has experienced pain or tension in their back and shoulders, or headaches. These are related to energy restriction along the spine in most cases. Problems in the arms, hands, hips and legs can be related to blockages here, as well. In fact, there are nerve centers coming from the spine that extend to every major area of the body. Keeping the energy of the spine open and balanced is quite a big deal! It can help so much in our body and in our emotional state, too.

Since most drawings of the chakra system show the energy centers on the front of the body, many people have come to believe that this is where they are located. However, the chakras anchor at the spine and their energy circulates through the front and the back of the body. There are also meridians that run the length of the body. These are similar to our nervous system or our blood vessels, except they carry our life force energy. There are energy storage centers along the route of these meridians that collect and hold energy for us. When the meridians are functioning well, energy flows as it needs to from one center to the other, connecting everything very nicely. We feel well and are healthy. But when difficulties arise, such as stress and negative emotions, these become blocked or sluggish. Reiki helps to clear these and open the flow back up.

When I do self-Reiki, I typically make a point to treat my back, paying particular attention to my spine and my kidneys. Not only does it feel warm and soothing, but I can feel the energy opening in my spinal column when I do this. It makes a huge difference in the way I feel. Yet it can sometimes be challenging to reach my spine, especially if I am experiencing a blockage which is creating restriction. This is precisely when I need treatment the most! So I recently developed a method to assist me with self-Reiki of the back. It works beautifully, so I am sharing it with you!

This is done in the shower with the assistance of the water flow. I typically do this at the end of my shower and it takes only a minute or so. If you don't have a shower, or if you prefer to do it without getting wet, you could simply visualize the water flowing.

1. Ground and drop into your body as you stand under the flow of the water, with your back to the shower spray. Allow the water to flow down the back of your head from the crown,

all the way down your spine. Ask the water to assist you in treating your spine.

2. Begin to imagine that the water is infused with Reiki. You could send Reiki to the shower head prior to beginning, if you like, or you can simply send love and Reiki to the water as it falls.

3. Imagine that the Reiki infused water is flowing into your head, through your brain and down your spinal column all the way to the base. You may see it become a color or it may appear as a column of bright light. Whatever you see (or don't see) is fine and perfect. It may change each time.

4. If you like and it is comfortable, place one hand on top of your head or at the top of your spine and the other hand at the base of your spine and allow Reiki to flow through the spinal column.

5. Finish by placing one hand on each kidney (on the back, under the ribs) and allow Reiki to flow. Ask the water to continue to assist by sending Reiki infused water to this area. When I do this, water naturally flows down my arms to the kidney area I am treating.

This feels wonderful, whether I do it in my morning shower, or at the end of a day when my back feels tight. I can feel the blockages release very quickly and see the energy flowing smoothly. I firmly believe that regularly treatment of the spinal area is so important, so I am happy to have found this.

Give it a try!

The Importance of Shadow Work

As energy workers and light workers, it can seem really tempting to keep our attention only on the aspects of ourselves that we like or that we feel are "spiritual" enough. We can feel tempted to resist the aspects of our personality that cause us to feel triggered, angry, sad, worried or fearful and to cling to the aspects of ourselves that feel happy. We may not want to admit that we get caught in judgment of others or that certain situations are overwhelming or unpleasant to us.

It is a trap to believe that being a spiritual person or a light worker means that we don't have any darkness or that we are supposed to pretend we are perfect or superhuman. When we don't acknowledge the aspects of ourselves that we reject or that we are ashamed of, we are not able to find complete acceptance. We are not able to fully see our own Higher Self and the Divine working through us, because we continue to believe we are separate and unworthy of being whole. We can only go so far on our healing path without truly looking within ourselves and examining the parts of ourselves we judge.

Shadow work, sometimes called healing the inner child, is the willingness to begin honestly noticing when you are triggered in some way in order to begin understanding why and how you respond the way you do. The point of this is not to explain away the trigger or to cling to your thoughts and emotions, but simply to observe what is happening within you in a non-judgmental way. By doing this, you can begin to learn more about your automatic reactions and what thoughts you have during emotional responses.

It is not possible to work entirely from alignment and truth if we are fragmented within ourselves. Yet, we all have aspects of ourselves that we don't want to acknowledge and we push away. Most of us have many parts of us that we deny. Each time we cling to something or push something away, we are meeting up with an aspect of ourselves that is fearful. When we examine and acknowledge that fear (and any other feelings), we may find that a part of us is ready to learn more about who we are. The more we can acknowledge the way we truly feel, while not clinging to it or pushing it away, the more we can release it without getting caught in automatic reactions. We can then choose to respond in the way that feels most in integrity to us at that time, without the confusion of remaining stuck in old thought patterns that don't work anymore.

To do shadow work, the next time you are triggered or feeling difficult emotional extremes:

1.   Practice breathing in your belly by noticing the breath rising and falling in your abdomen, especially the low belly. You may need to consciously let go of tension in the belly to really feel the breath move in and out. Many of us hold tension there, especially when we are upset or stressed.

2.   Notice your inner responses--how you think and feel, where you feel it in your body, what the triggers were. Notice any thoughts you may be having about the emotions or the situation. Note any constriction in your body.

3.   Honor your feelings without judgment or further reaction. Neither try to push them away, nor engage in thoughts, words or actions that build upon them. Simply

observe and allow the emotional energy to move through you. Continue to breathe. Speak to the feelings, if that feels comfortable to you.

4.   Note what your reaction has been to the emotion, again without judgment. How do you feel about the reaction? Is there constriction in your body when you think about this?

5.   Ask yourself if the thoughts you have been telling yourself about this emotion and this situation are really true? If you are afraid of something, ask yourself if you can be OK with that happening. Can you trust the Universe? Can you offer the situation to your Higher Self or the Divine?

6.   Can you step back, even a little bit, and see if there is a larger message that is available to you? Messages are available in any situation, particularly those we are triggered by. We only need to pay attention. These messages can come from our body, our environment, song lyrics, animals, etc. In fact, repeating situations themselves can be seen as messages that something within us is asking for attention and healing.

Shadow work can be challenging at times, but it is very rewarding work. The longer you do this work, the better you will understand yourself and your own place in the Universe. In addition, your need to judge others will fade. **The things**

we judge in others are often aspects of ourselves that we are not able to tolerate. As we heal and develop understanding and compassion for the many aspects of ourselves, we find that we have the same for others.

10 Ways to Fit Self Reiki into Your Day

One of the biggest things I see as a comment from other Reiki practitioners is that they can't find time to do daily self Reiki. Some say they don't do self Reiki at all because they don't have time. Schedules are demanding, for sure. So I wanted to make a list of 10 ways that might spark the imagination and get folks thinking of creative ways to fit the wonderful gift of self Reiki into their day, if only for a minute or two here and there. It makes such a difference!

1.   Do self Reiki as you fall asleep at night. No need to make it complicated. Simply place your hands wherever you feel led to that night and ask Reiki to flow. Allow yourself to drift off to sleep like this. Not only do many people find this

a simple way to fit Reiki into their day, it is an amazing way to fall asleep!

2.   Set an alarm to do self Reiki for a few minutes when you first wake up in the morning. Some people find they are more able to fit this in and it is a refreshing and relaxing way to start the day. You could make it part of a meditation routine, if you have one.

3.   Give yourself Reiki as you browse the internet.

4.   Watching TV or a movie is a very good time to do self Reiki. Take advantage of the fact that you are sitting still and relaxing to increase the relaxation.

5.   While you are waiting in line. Waiting in lines challenges our patience. So take the opportunity to strengthen yourself. Any line works. The bank, the take out place, a long line in traffic. Just one hand placed discreetly on yourself keeps you calm and gives you a dose of self Reiki.

6.   One of my personal favorites is while cuddling with someone. I place on hand on the person I am cuddling and one hand on myself and let the Reiki flow. We make a big Reiki healing loop and everyone benefits.

7.   Place one hand over each chakra for 3-5 deep breaths as you let Reiki flow. Do this as often as you have time.

8.   If you find you have no free hands and you still want to do a bit of self Reiki, you can simply ask Reiki to flow into you! If you are attuned, Reiki is already flowing through you. Ask for it to flow and notice how you feel in the top of your

head, your heart and your hands and feet. You may not always notice much, but very often you will feel tingling and warmth in these areas.

9.   Give yourself Reiki while you read! Whether it's a great story, a magazine, a textbook, or something online (even this article--hint, hint!), while you're reading is a great time to place a hand on yourself for Reiki.

10.   While outdoors in nature. This is a favorite time for me to take self Reiki. There are many ways to do it. Ask Reiki to flow as you walk. Sit under a tree and give yourself Reiki or simply ask it to flow. You may feel the energy of the tree, as well. Lay on the ground and do self Reiki, if you have time. I highly recommend doing this at least once. It is an amazing experience. Highly grounding and full of wonderful energy. Very healing.

Remember, the effects of Reiki are cumulative and its effects are often subtle! You have to keep doing it to see the biggest results, but the results are amazing in the long haul!

10 Ways to Use Reiki in Everyday Life

Reiki is not just something I practice on myself to stay well or on others to assist them in their well being. Reiki is an integral part of my life. It is something I acknowledge throughout my day, from the moment I wake up until I fall asleep at night. I see it as a vast and living energy that connects me, in a very real way that I can feel, to my Higher Power. I ask the Reiki energy to assist me, for the greatest and highest good, in most everything I do throughout my day. I understand it as a critical part of my spiritual path.

Here are some ways you can incorporate Reiki into your day. Use your creativity to see what other ways you can think of to invite this beautiful energy into your life.

1.   Infuse your intentions and prayers for the day with Reiki when you first wake up. Also consider doing self Reiki for a few minutes first thing in the morning.

2.   Send Reiki to your food as you make breakfast (or any meal) and also bless it as you sit down to eat the meal. You can send Reiki to your groceries when you harvest them from the garden or buy them at the store as well.

3.   Meditation is a wonderful time to tune in to the Reiki energy, allowing yourself to become more familiar with it or to allow the energy to flow to yourself for self-healing.

4.   When you leave for the day, take a moment to send Reiki to your car and to the trip ahead. You can also send Reiki to the destination you are headed to and to any situation you will be arriving into.

5.   Incorporate Reiki into any spiritual practices you have throughout the day, contemplating ways that this life force energy surrounds and interconnects us all. Think of how this understanding might affect your spiritual practices of compassion, kindness, forgiveness and gratitude.

6.   Most animals very much enjoy Reiki! It is often preferred from a distance, though your own pets may love it hands on. You can also treat their food, water, bedding and toys with Reiki.

7.   If you have houseplants, cut flowers or a garden, honor and nourish them as they honor you. Give them an energy exchange by offering them Reiki! It is also useful to treat their soil and water with Reiki.

8.   Use Reiki to cleanse and protect the energy of your home or work environment. Reiki chi balls are very useful for this. You can also use Reiki to quickly clear and charge your crystals.

9.   If you are having a difficult time or a conflict in a relationship, you can send Reiki to the situation and to yourself to help ease the difficult emotions and bring about a resolution to the issue.

10.   At the end of the day, you can send Reiki to your final prayers and to your sleep, asking that you be shown the resolution to any issues you are struggling with as you sleep.

Remember the Reiki precepts each day and practice using Reiki in as many ways as you can think of and you will soon find that it becomes a part of you. Your spiritual practice and Reiki will be intertwined and your life will be a spiritual practice. That doesn't mean you will be perfect, but you will see how to honor life and yourself in more ways all the time.

Strengthening Your Connection with Reiki

Sometimes practitioners worry that they are not feeling very much energy flowing through their hands or their bodies. This is a question I receive quite a bit. I would like to address this by offering a few suggestions for strengthening the ways with which you can feel your connection with and your understanding of Reiki.

Reiki will flow through your body differently according to how it is needed in each situation and your perceptions will change from time to time as well, so that needs to be taken into account going in. Also know that there is no need to fear that Reiki is not flowing. However, I do believe that, with practice, we can become more aware of how Reiki flows through us and works with our individual systems.

Practice One: Place your hands together in prayer position at the heart. Hold them there for several minutes and simply sense how the energy flows in your hands. Notice the palms or any fingers that offer any sensation. Don't look for something specific. Your sensations are your own. Simply notice what is there. Breathe and notice and keep returning your attention to this area for at least 2-3 minutes, extending to five or so minutes a day. You could also try placing your hands at the third eye in prayer position for a portion of the practice and see what sensations you notice in your hands.

Practice Two: Briskly rub your hands together for a minute or so. Now hold them in front of your body, palms facing each other, about an inch apart. Gently and slowly push the palms towards each other but don't quite let them touch. Do you feel the gentle pushing sensation between your hands? That is the energy in your body. You may also sense a tingling or a heat in the center of your palms, or not. Either way is fine. Now try gently and slowly pulling the hands away from each other. Do you feel how it seems as if you are pulling taffy? The hands seem to be pulling toward each other. You are sensing the magnetic field of the body. These are ways the energy works in the body. Reiki is a part of that and the more you can tune into this, the more you will understand about how Reiki works in your body.

Practice Three: Do self Reiki every single day. Fit it in every way you can, using one hand while you do something else, if you need to. This is beneficial in the sense that your system is getting Reiki. However, if you are having difficulty sensing Reiki flow and you want to understand it better, you really need to take at least ten minutes or more a day to devote solely to self Reiki, so that you can notice how the energy moves through you, both in your hands and as it flows through your body. The subtle sensations may be very difficult to notice if you aren't tuned in with your awareness. Use it as a body meditation. If you feel you are too busy, all the more reason to slow down for yourself, your peace of mind and to honor your practice for ten minutes a day. All practices take some commitment and all skills take practice. It may help you to keep a notebook keeping track of what you noticed in your body, heart, head and hands each day. You may also choose to note a few simple things that you were dealing with in your life, physically, mentally or emotionally, so that you can begin to notice the changes that regular Reiki practice brings about.

Practice Four: Use Reiki on others often. This gives you a chance to notice the differences in the ways that Reiki flows with each person and each situation. Also, use Reiki in different life situations in everyday life. Use it on your food, in your bath, on your bed, your car before driving, everywhere you can think of! Practice, practice, practice!

Connecting with Your Guides

Long before I first heard of Reiki, I was aware of guides in my life. I had been aware of guides and spirits since my earliest childhood memories. However, I found early on that most people either were not aware of their own guides or were not comfortable talking about them, so I learned to stop discussing them and eventually began to wonder if something was wrong with me for experiencing these loving presences. I pushed them to the background as I grew up and went on with the business of making my way in the world.

Later, after a near death experience, the encounters came to the forefront again. I still refused to talk about them with others, fearing even more what would be determined about my state of mental stability. However, I was grateful for their guidance and their love. They always radiated complete love and peace, like nothing I had felt before, except from them and in the space between life and death. Their guidance was always kind and it was always helpful. I didn't always listen or understand the guidance, but I learned to ask questions when I didn't understand, just as you would with a tender and gentle teacher.

I have since come to know many other people who admit to knowing their own guides and trusting them as wise counselors and friends. It no longer seems like such a strange idea to me to be open about this, yet I am aware that for many this is a taboo subject that speaks of "dark magic" or mental illness.

I also know that not everyone is aware of their guides. I believe we all have them, some of us simply may not be tuned in or may be expecting to receive a connection in the same way as others do. Our brains are all unique and we each receive information in different ways. Some may receive information from their guides through visual stimulation in the mind, with images appearing in the mind's eye or perceiving things in their environment more clearly than others. Others may receive sounds very clearly in their ears or as words in their heads. Some may receive a sudden *"knowing"*, very clear information about something they have no previous knowledge about. There are many ways to receive information and some receive in a combination of these.

You do not need to be connected to or aware of your guides to practice Reiki. Sometimes new practitioners become very concerned that this hasn't happened for them. Chances are, you are receiving information and you simply aren't aware of it. There is no need to worry about being a *"bad"* practitioner or that you aren't spiritual enough if you aren't aware of your guides! You are fine!

You can keep setting the intention that you would like to connect with your guides, in the way that is most appropriate for you. Ask that any blocks or fears you have about receiving information from guides be removed as well. When the time is right, it will happen. Be open to it and be open to the manner in which it may happen. Relax.

Try keeping a dream journal, as messages often comes through both our subconscious and our guides in the form of dreams. Writing down your dreams can be a valuable way to see what your dreams are telling you. You may also benefit from taking note of any instances in waking life where you felt inexplicably drawn or led to do something. What happened when you did this? Or what were the results when you resisted?

Don't get stuck on expecting to see a person appear in front of you. Not everyone has this experience. And not every experience with the same guide will be like that, even if it is sometimes. In my experience, when I have "*seen*" guides I saw them in my mind's eye, not with my physical ones and they were not like physical people. They were beings of light. They were auras that emanated light, especially from their hearts.

Whether you think of guides as actual beings, as your Higher Self, your subconscious mind, as God or as intuition, it really makes no difference in the end. It is receiving information from a part of you or through a part of you that is capable of seeing and understanding things in a different and more expansive way. If this is helpful and loving, then why not make use of it? There is also no need to banish logical thinking. A good balance of intuition and logic makes for a balanced mind and a more functional life. Embrace your whole mind, logic and intuition.

Healing Your Home and Your Environment

We can use Reiki and healing energy to bring cleansing, strength/protection and healing into our homes, our work spaces and even extend it out into our neighborhoods. I often use this technique during and after an illness in the house, after an argument or a bad mood has happened, and before and after guests visit. Anytime your home begins to feel energetically heavy and dense or you sense tension and upset is a good time to use this technique or something similar to clear the energy in your space. It is also helpful when you know you could use a boost of strength, such as when a big storm is coming. I will write another article specifically about using Reiki for storm protection very soon as this works very well.

First, sit or stand somewhere comfortable in your home and take a few deep, cleansing breaths to center yourself. Ask the Healing Energy of the Universe to assist you in bringing strength, cleansing and healing to your home and all beings live there. Intend that all that does not belong be cleared away. Call upon the strength of the directions--North, South, East and West, above, below, within. Ask the elements that are the basis of all life to support you--Earth, Air, Water, Fire, Ether. Call upon any guides that feel appropriate to you.

Next, Envision the Power Symbol (CKR) and draw it in the air with your hand, if you like. Then begin making a chi ball in front of your body, about the size of a soccer ball. Roll this energy ball between your hands and begin to feel the energy build as you envision the Power Symbol (CKR), the Mental/Emotional Symbol (SHK) and the Distant Symbol (HSZSN), infusing the chi ball with their energies. Once this chi ball feels complete, give it a push toward the North facing wall of your home with the intention that it infuse its energies into it, clearing and healing as it goes. Repeat this step with the South facing wall, East, West and then do the same with the floor and the ceiling.

After you have infused all directions, the floor and ceiling of your space with healing chi balls, form another one in the same manner. This new one will be directed specifically into yourself and it will amplify your own healing, strengthening, and cleansing. Once you have formed the chi ball, push it into your heart center and envision it radiating outward from there, filling you with all of the symbols. Imagine CKR, in particular, filling each cell, each molecule until they are now radiating a glowing and healthy light. Imaging that all that needs to be cleansed and released is easily letting go from each cell, each molecule and all is coming back into balance. You may notice pain releasing, or things popping loose as energy frees itself. Allow yourself to sit peacefully and rest, feeling this warm sensation for as long as you like.

Bonus Exercise: If you choose to keep going, you can continue clearing energy in your home and even your neighborhood in much the same way. Simply allow the image of CKR to continue to radiate outward from your heart center, infusing cells and molecules. Know that it will be just as healing to whatever you infuse it into as it feels when you infuse it into yourself. You can envision and intend that healing energy in CKR infuse the molecules in the structure of your building, the trees on your property, each blade of grass, the neighbor's homes, the soil, your car, even molecules of the air. The possibilities are endless! Let the energy and your creativity guide you.

Healing Your Family Ancestry

We understand that we are physically affected by our family ancestry through our DNA and mentally through our parent's influence on us during our upbringing, but it goes much deeper than that and carries much further through time and space than we tend to realize. The DNA and the decisions of relatives we never even met echoes through us and those ripples still continue to affect us until they are healed and the waves are calmed once more. Indeed, they will continue to ripple through our lives and even through the lives of our children and grandchildren until the healing is complete.

For example, we all have seen how abuse can carry on from generation to generation, even if it doesn't carry itself out in the same way. Sometimes it will be a husband who abuses his spouse, and the next generation it may be the daughter allowing herself to be abused by her husband, abusing herself or even her children. In the next generation, the cycle will continue in a new, yet familiar way. It doesn't stop until someone is able to recognize a new way and heal the pattern in their mind, their heart and their family. The same is true for cycles of abandonment, poverty, war, religious zeal and many other things. Or for any unhealed pattern or illness in a family line, physical or otherwise.

But how do we heal the patterns in the minds or DNA of family members we may have never met, from our long distant past? Or from far into the future? How can we heal our present family situation when we feel so deeply involved in the outcome?

When we notice a pattern arising in ourselves, particularly if it is one that repeats in similar ways in members of our family, whether it is with a health issue or a negative behavior pattern, then we can send healing to the entire family line, starting with ourselves and echoing outward. So, in the same way that the illness or damaging pattern echoes out through space and time, we will echo healing energy out through space and time, through all the DNA, molecules, mental, emotional and auric layers of our family ancestry.

To do this, relax and take a few deep breaths as you focus on the pattern or illness that you wish to send healing energy to. Try not to get too emotionally caught up in the outcome of the healing and simply allow the energy to flow. Activate *Cho Ku Rei, Sei He Ki* and *Hon Sha Ze Sho Nen*, and intend that the healing flow throughout all of space and time, to any and all family members affected by this illness or damaging behavior pattern. Visualize the DNA of any who need the healing energy being infused with its light. See their neural pathways shifting and opening to allow for new understandings that will make healthy patterns possible. See the healing energy flowing through their minds and bodies, infusing their cells, flowing through every direction of time and space. Imagine any damage that has been done, now being healed and any lessons that were needed, now have been learned, all flowing in with the healing energy.

Once you feel this is complete for this session, close the session by sending a final boost of CKR through time and space through the family line, past, present and future. Try not to be too focused on a particular need or desire for a specific person or outcome. Instead, just allow the healing echo to continue to ripple throughout time and space as it needs to, trusting that it will find its way where it needs to go, much as water flows into the spaces it must fill.

Healing Past Wounds

We all have things in our past that have caused us pain or trauma. Some of these things can be quite severe and leave lingering effects or keep us living in the past, either reliving the wound or wishing for what we believe should have happened instead. This keeps us stuck, unable to move forward and enjoy our lives in the moment or create the future we would like to live. These painful memories and stuck traumas also tend to manifest in physical ways in our lives through repeating patterns we create without realizing it and through our bodies as physical illnesses.

We can make a big difference in our own lives and the lives of those around us by beginning to do conscious healing work on our past traumas. Each time you notice an emotion that repeatedly resurfaces around an old issue, you are wishing something could have turned out another way or feeling indignation or anger at the way something in the past went, you are likely stuck in an old painful memory. The same may be true if you find that something in the present makes you feel intense anxiety, fear or anger when there is no immediate threat of danger or loss to you.

Pay attention to your body signals when these things happen. Do you feel tight in your chest, throat or belly? Is your jaw clenched and your forehead bunched? Use all of these signs to notice that healing work needs to be done around the issue at hand. If it has gone on a long time, you will likely feel that the emotions are "justified" and you "have a right" to feel that way. You may use this to fan the flames of the emotion and make it stronger. Your feelings are your own and they are telling you that you need to be healed. They are not wrong or right. They are simply a signal.

When you have pinpointed the painful memory you are feeling stuck in, write it down on a piece of paper. Go into as much detail as you feel you need to, or simply use a few keywords that symbolize the memory for you. If you are also finding yourself stuck on playing out what you feel "should" have happened, write that down, too, preferably on a separate piece of paper. Again, use great detail, if that feels right, or a few symbolic keywords. Once you have these accounts written down, hold the memory of what actually happened in your hands and send it healing energy, love and gratitude. Send any healing symbols that feel intuitively appropriate to you. Hold it to your heart chakra as you extend gratitude to the person you are today for helping the person you were then to heal. Send deep love to all versions of yourself, at all ages.

Next, hold the account of what you wish would have happened in your hands. Begin sending healing energy, love and gratitude to what actually is as you allow yourself to let go of this false past. Allow yourself to see that it is not a true past and to grieve it fully so you can release it. It is OK to feel whatever comes up. That is part of the release and the healing. It has been dear to you and it's natural to grieve. Keep sending love to yourself and allowing what really is, knowing that what is now is OK. You can be in the present more fully without tending to a false past. Heal it completely and let it go.

Once you are done, either bury or burn (in a safe place where nothing will catch fire!) the pieces of paper, allowing healing energy to release the memories completely as you symbolically give them up to the elements. Again, use *Cho Ku Rei*, *Sei He Ki*, and /or *Hon Sha Ze Sho Nen* or any other symbols that you feel are appropriate. Spend a few additional minutes simply being aware of your breath, your body sensations and your energy field. You will likely feel a sense of lightness and freedom; however, you may feel somewhat drained and tired as well. Rest if you need to and drink plenty of water to help flush toxins. Do this process as often as necessary and recommend it to your clients, as well.

Sending Healing to Future Versions of Ourselves

We think a lot about sending healing or comfort to people and situations that are currently in pain, ill or in crisis. And there are lots of articles on Reiki Rays about ways to send healing to the past, including several that I have written myself. One thing that may not come up as often is sending healing to the future. Yet energy is not bound by time and space or the way that we envision circumstances unfolding. With energy, there are multitudes of ways that situations can unfold, beyond what we can comprehend.

We know we can send healing to the future for improving the outcome of potentially unpleasant events, such as surgeries, root canals and job interviews, and many of us practiced with this during or after Reiki Level 2 training. Yet it is possible to expand this so that you are sending Reiki ahead to all possible future versions of yourself. That sounds a little trippy, so let me explain.

When we use Reiki throughout time and space, we do it with the understanding that there are multiple possible outcomes on every path. We are not the only ones that decide how the path will go, though our intention, energy and actions certainly influence it. However, so do the intentions, energy and actions of many others. Reiki can offer the best outcome available, for the highest good of all.

With this in mind, we can send Reiki to all the possible paths. We don't need to know what they are, we only need ask Reiki to flow to them. We let ourselves be completely open to allowing the energy to bring about the best outcomes.

Here's how you can send a boost to your future

1.   Allow your mind to become calm and quiet in whatever way you choose. Meditation works well, as do breathing exercises. It can also be helpful to gaze into a candle flame to still your mind and bring focus.
2.   Notice your energy. It may be stronger in your low belly, your heart or between your eyes.
3.   Let your focus settle there and allow the energy to build as you connect with Reiki healing energy.
4.   Next, ask this energy to flow to all possible paths in your future, strengthening the best possible outcome for all. You might ask that you be supported and guided to the best possible way for you, and that you have the clarity to see the correct choices when they arrive. Invite inspiration and love.

This definitely brings changes in your life. However, we can block our own way, so in order for the benefits to be recognized and accepted in your life, there are a few things that you need to do to help.

1.   **Remember that you are energy, too.** Include your own self, your heart, mind and body, in the healing. Be open to loving yourself unconditionally, right where you are in this moment. It is your present self that is sending healing and love to your future self, so be sure to include your present self in this gift, rather than seeing the future as a place to get to. You are creating your future, so do it with love and from love.

2.   **After you have sent the healing energy, try not to cling to specifics about how it will unfold.** While is can be helpful to visualize how you would like to feel and what experiences you might like to have, it is best to keep the details generalized. When we mentally grasp hold of details, we don't leave room for other possibilities, which are often far better than we could have imagined.

3.   **As you go about your day, stay open and aware of how the energy is opening new paths to you.** See all the ways that the support, guidance, clarity and love that you asked for are arriving in your life. That may mean being flexible in how you expected things to go, at times. If we are always trying to force things to go the way we expect them to go, we aren't allowing the Universe to bring us to new paths! Doing things the same way and never being open only leaves us with the same repeating results.

You can do the exercise for a few moments each morning and evening, or just a couple times a week when you can give it your full focus. Remember to express gratitude for the new gifts that come in. Gratitude is a powerful creative energy that sends out the message that you are on the right track and wish to continue.

Using Reiki to Love Your Body

There is a huge push in the world media for everyone to lose weight, be fit, and be the correct size for the current fashion. It can begin to make you feel terrible about yourself, as if there is some specific impossible standard that remains somewhat (or drastically) out of reach for many of us. There are so many diets and fitness programs and many people, particularly women, are constantly on a new diet. We are conditioned to compare our bodies with those of others, and especially with those in magazines, movies and television.

All of this isn't a very loving way to live within our bodies. In fact, it sends negative messages and negative energy to our cells and creates negative thought processes in our minds. We reinforce this negative energy and these negative beliefs by continuing the cycle. And negative energy makes for a sick and toxic body that can't balance itself and heal. That is exactly the opposite of what we need when we want our body to feel its best!

We need to move our bodies in a way that makes us happy and that helps our energy and fluids to circulate well. And of course, we all need to eat food that supports our health, rather than diminishes it. But both food and movement should be supportive and joyous! Filling food and exercise with guilt and angst destroys the positive qualities of eating and moving! Choose how you need to eat and move based on what makes you and your body feel your very best—not on guilt laden messages or comparisons with others.

Of course what all of us really wish for is to feel our best. We want a body that will help us to move through this life freely, easily, and without pain. The truth is, that will look very different for each of us. And if we feel our best and we are happy, we will certainly look our best, too. The wonderful thing is, once you switch your internal program to one of love and acceptance, your cells will respond. You will feel better and be happier.

So how do we begin to change the programming we have learned?

1.   **Send Reiki directly to the cells of your body each day.** Make it a part of your self-Reiki or your meditation routine. Do this with the intention to deeply love and accept your body, just as it is. Try to really feel the energy of love in your heart center, the way you would feel it for a loved one or a favorite memory.

2.   **If there is a part of your body that you have particular difficulty feeling good about, spend a few extra moments sending Reiki and loving intention to this area.** This can be

an area that you have had feelings of self-loathing toward due to the way it looks or it can be an area that has pain or other difficulty.

3.   **You may notice that you carry feelings of guilt in your body.** Take note of where you carry the emotional energy of guilt. Spend some time breathing and letting Reiki flow to this area and sending loving intention and acceptance to it.

4.   **Set the intention to begin having a loving relationship with your food.** Allow Reiki to flow into this intention. Writing this down may be helpful.

5.   **Each time you eat, allow Reiki and loving energy to flow to your body and to the food you choose.** Bless it with positive energy prior to eating it. It is helpful to do this prior to going to the grocery store, the restaurant or the kitchen, as well. This places a loving bond of energy between you and your food.

6.   **If you currently have no exercise or physical movement routine, set the intention to explore new ways of movement that feel good to your body.** Write this down so that you can see the intention and so that you have a place to explore ideas. Be creative and write down several ways to move your body that sound fun and interesting. Any form of movement is good! Nothing is taboo, weird, or wrong. Make something up if you like! You could consider dancing of any kind (belly dancing could be fun!), hula hooping, walking

around the block, yoga or simple stretching, whatever moves you and feels good! Send Reiki and loving energy to this.

7. **Each day, choose a form of movement from your list to try for at least 5 minutes and send Reiki to the movement in advance.** You can do the exercise for as long as you like, but commit to at least starting and doing a few minutes. Ground into the Earth before beginning, thank your body and enjoy! Spend a moment at the end to place your hands over you heart and let Reiki flow. Thank your body once more for supporting you in this fun activity which strengthens you.

8. **Spend a moment or so in front of the mirror each day sending Reiki and love to your body.** Accept and appreciate it just as it is. Do not try to change it. Just love it.

The wonderful thing is, by loving and accepting ourselves just as we are, we free our minds and our cells to make the changes they need to. We allow healing and rebalancing toward health to take place.

Reiki to Heal Limiting Beliefs

As we grow up, we take on the beliefs of our parents, our culture, our religious teachers and our government and so on. Everything around us implants new ideas about how we are meant to think, feel and act. This is called socializing and it is needed to a certain degree in order for us to know how to function among those around us. We learn what is needed to remain safe.

Some of these beliefs are very functional in our immediate family or our local community. They can serve us very well. However, there are many beliefs that we learn that worked very well for our parents that don't serve us very well in the world today. Other things we learn may have served an important function in our lives while we were younger but no longer fit the person or life we have developed for ourselves. The world continues to change and grow and so do we.

When we subconsciously hold onto a belief that doesn't fit us, we become energetically stuck. At a deep level, our true being experiences the conflict between where we are in life and the beliefs we hold. Energy cannot flow unrestricted in a pathway held tight from conflict. We feel bad emotionally, mentally, spiritually and ultimately we will feel pain or sickness in our physical body.

It is important to remember that we are energetic beings. Every level of our energy system holds information for us about what we have experienced and how it has impacted us—negatively or positively. The spirit or soul is the level that remembers why we are here in physical form and guides us to the things that are for our greatest good and away from things that are leading away from it. Even things that lead us away from our highest good can be redirected to serve our highest good as we are never damaged permanently at the soul level.

When we use Reiki to heal ourselves or others, we are bringing the mental, emotional, physical and spiritual levels into more balanced alignment with each other. The Reiki flows through the energy pathways in the body helping to open up any restrictions, congestion and blockages in the energetic systems. One of the things Reiki can assist with in this process is releasing beliefs and thoughts that are causing a conflict with our lives and easing the restriction these beliefs have created. New ways of understanding the world can then come online to help us function in a way that is healthier for us.

If you want to use Reiki to help yourself release stale and limiting beliefs, the symbols can assist you in this. They are able to help you work more deeply on a mental and emotional level and also allow you to work without the limits of time and space to heal the past. It can also help to have a list of the beliefs you want to release.

Before you make your list of limiting beliefs, send Reiki to the process with the intent that you uncover the beliefs that are most restricting your self-healing right now. As you make the list, notice that certain beliefs trigger more emotion than others do. Make a special note by those that create emotional reactions. These are the ones that you need the most assistance in healing. Choosing to give yourself a Reiki treatment with the specific intent to release these beliefs can be very helpful in letting it go and healing.

Before you begin your self-treatment, set the specific intention that you release beliefs that do not serve you. Draw the Power symbol on both hands and over your head. Use the Mental and Emotional Healing symbol over your head. Then use the Distant symbol in order to heal anything from the past in connection with these beliefs. Repeat the Power symbol after this. Then begin your self-Reiki session. As you treat yourself, notice any feelings or thoughts that arise. Do not judge yourself for anything that comes up. Be very compassionate and gentle. Allow yourself to relax and let the Reiki flow through your energetic system, healing and repairing.

After doing this, you will begin to notice that your thoughts and feelings are changing. This process can feel uncomfortable at first. Remember that these old beliefs are all linked together and as one releases, others will need to alter to accommodate the process. Pay attention to the emotions this brings up as the healing continues after treatment. Remind yourself that you don't need to change anything you don't want to. Soon you will notice that you are feeling more in tune with yourself and making decisions that fit more with who you truly are.

Release Ceremony

Thoughts and emotional energy can sometimes race through our minds, running in a never-ending loop that is not helpful, but difficult to let go of. Or we may notice issues, relationships or beliefs we wish to be done with or wish to deal with in a healthier way. When we are feeling heavy and weighed down emotionally or physically and can't seem to easily re-set, we can perform a cleansing and releasing ceremony.

Ceremonies such as this one can powerfully release the old and re-set out intentions in the direction we mean to go, without old baggage weighing us down. I love doing this ceremony regularly, even if I am not feeling any difficulty, simply because it is so beautiful and reaffirming. It is lovely to do on the full moon, or at the equinoxes or solstices.

In order to do this ceremony, you will need the following:

•   A candle or candles. White ones are good to represent cleansing and purity, but you can also choose red to represent release and fire purification, or blue to represent protection and air or water purification or green to represent healing and earth purification. Purple may feel best for you, to represent the Violet Flame. Choose any color that resonates with you.

•   Incense or sage.

•   Bath tub or shower. A tub is best, but this can be adapted to work in a shower, if you use your imagination. Your intention and the work with the Divine energy through the elements is the important thing.

•   Sea salt or Epsom salts to add to bath. You can add herbs or flowers, as well. Rose petals or basil can be very healing and purifying.

•   Essential oils are a nice bonus, but not critical.

To perform the ceremony, follow these steps:

1.   **Cleanse your ceremonial space and your aura** using either incense or sage. Ask that the smoke purify anything that doesn't belong to you any longer. Make sure to sweep the smoke through all areas of the room, including corners. Then pass the smoke through your aura, starting at your head and working your way down to your feet. Sweep down one arm and then the other. When you are finished, you can put the

incense out in a bowl of sea salt or water, or allow it to continue burning as you perform your ceremony.

2.   **Draw your bath and add salt**, and herbs or flowers, if using. Charge the water with Reiki.

3.   **Light the candles** while the water is running, saying a prayer over them as you do. Ask for assistance from all elements, angels, and guides that serve the Divine to help you release the weight of what weighs you down and no longer serves you, releasing any cords and healing both ends with love and forgiveness. Charge the candles with Reiki, using all symbols that you are guided to.

4.   **As you undress, imagine you are removing layers of what is weighing you down**, releasing it to the Earth. Thank the Earth for her help in transmuting this for you and ask her to bless all beings with the transmuted energy.

5.   **Step into the tub** and see the water beginning to dissolve what remains. Ask it to assist you as you do your healing ceremony.

6.   Use your hand to **scoop handfuls of the water over your crown**, letting it pour over your third eye and over the back of your head and down your spine. Do this at least 3 times, feeling the water cleanse and heal you, removing what doesn't belong. Do this at least once over each chakra. See the water as both purifying water doesn't belong, and replenishing what does.

7.   **Rest back into the water and close your eyes**. You may wish to let yourself sink into the water as far as you can go while still being able to breathe. Begin to meditate, allowing any thoughts, feelings or issues that would like to release rise to the surface. See them and thank them, then let them go. Do this for as long as you feel you need to. Remember you have the service of your guides, angels and elements to assist you. If something feels difficult, you are fully supported in its release, if it is what you choose.

8.   **When you feel complete**, sit up, thank the water for assisting you releasing and transmuting these things and ask it to bless all beings it touches, and all water everywhere as it flows away from you. Open the drain and step out.

9.   **Look into your eyes in the mirror** and gently remind yourself that you are a much loved and supported child of the Divine.

10.   **If you are using essential oils**, you can anoint your hands, feet and each chakra, setting the intention that you will walk in the Divine Christed Light, allowing Divine Will to work through you as a peaceful channel. You can anoint using a symbol or simply draw a cross. Intention is what is important.

When you are finished with your ceremony, you may feel very tired. If so, please rest as long as you need to. Drink plenty of water over the next 24 hours to help flush away all that you have broken free. You may notice that you urinate more in the hours immediately following the ceremony, as well. This ceremony will produce shifts and healing. The precise results will vary each time, according to what you may need in that instance, but you will notice an immediate shift.

Healing Your Relationships with Receiving

One thing that has become more and more clear to me as I walk my path of spiritual growth and awareness is that we are literally surrounded by all that we need, always. We are amazing transmitters of energy and conduits to receive energy into our being as well. Information is constantly going in and out of our fields, a non-stop communication transmission between us and the Universe. The truth is, most of us have very little or no awareness that this communication is happening.

Yet, our beliefs, thought patterns, habits, emotional patterns and intentions all send out signals to the Universe regarding what we want, don't want, need and don't need in our lives. They express what we are ready to take on and what we have not yet learned ways to handle. We then receive experiences that match the frequency we are sending out.

Often when we are not living the life we want to live or our life is filled with obstacles or lack, we begin to blame outside forces, such as another person or just "bad luck". We can tend to fall into believing we are a victim of the Universe, rather than an active participant in what we ask for and receive. This then becomes another belief system that influences the signal that your energy sends out. That belief will be reinforced in your experiences until you decide to question its validity.

Many spiritual leaders, including Jesus, have taught us that we are co-creators with the Universe by way of sending out signals that then bring in what we need. "Ask and you shall receive," is an example. There is also much mention of doubt being a stumbling block and belief, or faith, being the path to creating what you desire. This speaks to a shift in your understanding of how the energy system works within the Universe and how your thoughts, beliefs, intentions and emotions affect it.

If you wish to create a better awareness of this process, one of the first things to do is to simply ask that the blocks that you have to seeing and understanding the process be dissolved or removed. Set an intention for this every day and pray or meditate with this intention as your specific focus for a few minutes. This is very important, because we will not see the process at work until the beliefs that block it from our sight are gone. Don't try to force the process, simply allow it to happen.

Next, you can begin setting intentions for manifestations. You can start very small, if you like, or go much bigger. I feel that it helps to set an intention for a larger manifestation and then "practice" every day with small ones to build your confidence. Focus on the way you wish to feel, rather than on the precise material path you believe you will take to get to that feeling. Envision yourself in that setting. See what's around you as you feel this desired emotion. Don't ask for things you don't really want!

Keep in mind that small manifestations don't take as long to show up as very large ones. A large manifestation, such as a new business, will require energy to shift and reshape in the material realm on many levels and various areas in order to manifest. And it will likely also require shifts in your thinking and your beliefs, and perhaps a few lessons that you need in order to be able to have the knowledge to handle the request. A smaller manifestation, such as seeing a particular bird or a butterfly, is something that can happen fairly quickly. As you practice, you may find these small things happen almost immediately after your request.

Always be open to how the manifestation will be given to you by the Universe. You can't see the whole picture, so allow the Universe to do the work from a higher perspective, without insisting that it go your way. You may only create new blocks by being willful about the precise way it manifests.

Express gratitude in advance, and each time you notice something falling into place as the manifestation begins coming into view. Gratitude sends out a loving energy that creates an open channel for more to be received. A simple way to open a channel for abundance to flow using gratitude is through blessing your money and your bills. Before paying your bills, send Reiki to them, being grateful for whoever supplied you with that service and for the money you have to pay for it. Send Reiki blessings to whoever you received the money from as well, and ask that all that the money touches receive a blessing, creating a lovely ripple effect.

Chapter 3 – Chakras

Chakras and Meridians

When learn about how the physical body works, we learn that there are organs throughout the body and that there are blood vessels and nerve endings that carry life force and information all around the body, to and from these organs. We learn that these processes keep us alive and healthy. We learn that when these processes become stagnant or blocked, through age, injury or disease, we become ill or we die. These things are all true. And there is more.

The energy in our bodies also moves through a system that in some ways resembles the organs and the pathways of the blood vessels and nerves. This system functions as a way to help keep our energy flowing efficiently, so that we stay well. We can also relate it to the electricity that flows through our homes. There is an energy system, pathways and switch points to direct the current properly.

The meridians are the pathways in our bodies through which our energy (also called chi, prana, ki, life force or spirit) flows. Much like our blood vessels, when these pathways are clear and open, we feel good and we are well. But in the same way that we can have a heart attack or stroke when our blood vessels become blocked, when our meridians become blocked we feel fatigue, sickness, pain or mental unbalance. Negative emotions, stress and trauma cause blockage in our meridians and must be cleared in some way in order to prevent or relieve illness or imbalance.

The chakras are major energy centers in the body. They are the body's energy "organs". They transmit and receive large amounts of energy and information to and from our environment. The chakras also send information within the body through the meridian system. They spin in a vortex or funnel shape, with the center of the funnel connecting at the spine.

When the energy in the body becomes slowed or blocked, the chakras don't spin as well. Imagine if you had an electrical wire in your home that was disconnected or if you had a fuse that was out. In the same way that your lights, computers and appliances would not work, your body can't work properly when its energy flow is slowed or blocked. Reiki opens up the meridians (the wires), sending healthy energy flowing through the chakras (the fuses) again.

There are many chakras in the body. Seven of them are considered to be major chakras by most energy healing systems.

The **Root/Base chakra** is at the base of the spine in the area of the perineum. It is related to survival and grounding. It is associated with the color red.

The **Sacral chakra** is located in the lower part of the belly, about 2 inches below the navel. It is related to sexual relations, children and your sense of purpose. It is associated with the color orange.

The **Solar Plexus chakra** is located midway between the sternum and the navel. It is related to self esteem and processing emotions. When you feel a "gut reaction", it is the chakra you are experiencing. It is associated with the color yellow.

The **Heart chakra** is located directly in the center of the chest, over the sternum. It is related to love, compassion, sharing and the ability to connect.

The **Throat chakra** is located in the neck, from the upper chest to the mouth. It is related to creativity, communication and expressing oneself. It is associated with the color blue.

The **Third Eye chakra** is located in the center of the forehead, between the eyes, above the nose. It is associated with intuition, imagination, insight, psychic abilities and the unconscious mind. It is related to the color indigo.

The **Crown chakra** is located at the top of the head. It is associated with a spiritual connection to the Divine, understanding your oneness with all things and bliss. It is related to the color purple.

Other chakras are those in the hands and feet, which healers are often more aware of, since we feel them heat up and tingle when we do healing work. Healers may also feel heat, mild pressure and other sensations in their Crown and Heart chakras while doing healing work as the Reiki energy flows through these energy centers as it works.

Chakras Intensive

Part 1- Lower Chakras

Recently I wrote about the Chakras and Meridians, which was a basic explanation of the body's energy system. In this article I will go into more detail about the chakras, how we experience them in our bodies in our daily lives and how we might experience them if they were not functioning well. Reiki always works to balance all the chakras.

The **Root Chakra** is located at the base of the spine, near the perineum. Imagine an upside down funnel whose neck connects to the base of the spine right between the legs. The opening of the funnel opens and extends downward, encompassing the legs and feet.

We experience energy in this chakra when we are feeling very safe and rooted, or when we feel fearful. You may notice that when you feel this way, you feel strongly supported in your legs, or a magnetized sensation in the feet. This is being grounded.

When we feel frightened or unsafe, we may feel "weak-kneed", as if we need to sit down, or we may freeze in our tracks, unable take another step.

The root chakra is very important as it supports our entire physical system, including the blood, the muscular-skeletal system, the immune system, the lower intestines, legs, feet and the skin. It also supports our individuality, courage and learning to be stable.

When it is not functioning well, we may have issues with our knees, feet, legs, skin, blood, muscles or bones or have frequent injuries. Life issues may include being fearful or insecure, money problems (lack or greed), hoarding, blaming, anger and violence, or holding things in, tension or constipation.

Gardening or other outdoor activities, as well as food and sleep help to balance the root chakra.

The **Sacral Chakra** is located about two inches below the navel.

We experience energy moving in this chakra when we feel the tugging or the tingly butterflies sensation in our lower belly. These sensations are often related to sexual attraction or orgasm, feelings of maternal attachment or concern, or the feeling of pursuing our purpose in life. The sacral chakra supports the genitals, reproductive organs, intestines and bladder. It also supports our creative ability, our connection and healthy boundaries in interpersonal relationships, our personal purpose and it is our center for processing pleasure in this world.

When it is not functioning well we may have issues in our intestines, our uterus and/or ovaries, our prostate, testes or genitalia, spleen or bladder. We may also have difficulty opening ourselves up in a relationship or have issues with possessiveness or jealousy. There may also be imbalances relating to food or sex, such as an eating disorder (anorexia or overeating), sexual obsession, impotence or lack of desire. Fertility problems are often related to a blockage in the sacral chakra of one or both partners.

Swimming or other water activities, as well as activities that make use of creativity and the senses, such as dance or exercise are balancing for this chakra.

The **Solar Plexus Chakra** is located midway between the sternum and the navel.

We experience energy moving in this chakra when we have a "gut reaction" to something. When you are doing something that you know is wrong for you, you will feel a clenching or flipping feeling in your upper belly, or maybe you feel a burning there instead. Most of us feel something there when a situation is wrong for us. There is also slight feeling of lift and lightness in the same area when something feels right for us, making us feel happy, whole and complete. For this reason, this is also where we experience sensation most when we laugh and we are likely to experience some sensation here with most strong emotions.

The solar plexus governs the pancreas, liver, kidneys, gallbladder, stomach, adrenals and greatly supports the nervous system. It also supports our personal power in the world, our will and how we function and conduct ourselves. This is where we master our emotions, desire and energy, either making good use of them or turning them into destructive forces. It helps us with responsibility and choosing appropriate action.

When the solar plexus is not functioning well we tend to have digestive issues affecting the pancreas, liver, gallbladder or stomach, though the kidneys and adrenals may also be affected. We may also have problems in taking on too much, driving ourselves too hard, having an intense focus on recognition or power. A person having problems in this chakra may be competitive, domineering and overly full of energy or they may be the opposite and have low self-esteem, very little will or drive and a low energy level.

Finding ways that help you to face your fears or anger or otherwise safely and constructively express your emotions, such as journaling or communicating to loved ones or yelling into a pillow help to balance and heal this chakra. Laughter and inner self nurturing are needed as well.

Part 2 - Middle Chakras

The **Heart Chakra** is located in the center of the chest, anchoring right over the sternum.

We experience the heart chakra as a warm throbbing pull when we feel a deep loving connection to someone. We might say they "tug on our heartstrings" because we feel a sensation in our chest as a feeling of love. We also feel energy in this chakra as a crushing, burning pain when we experience deep loss or grief, such as when a relationship breaks up or someone close to us dies or is very ill. We often call this "heartache" because it truly does hurt in our chest. The heart chakra is a major energy center, which connects us in many ways to all of our other energy centers and connects our upper chakras to the lower chakras. We will feel energy moving here in many situations. Such as a lightness and an openness when we are feeling happy. Or a constriction when we are feeling stressed and anxious.

The heart chakra affects the heart, lungs, thymus, arms and hands. It also supports our ability to love ourselves and others, have compassion and empathy, be content and at peace, have trust, to be non-judgmental and to be accepting of ourselves, others and what is.

When it is not functioning well, we may have issues with the heart, lungs, circulatory system, immune system, arms or hands (including injury). Life issues may include fear of showing love or repression of love, martyrdom, jealousy, codependency, excessive focus on people pleasing, being withdrawn or isolating, being critical or intolerant of others and lacking empathy. People who are wounded in the heart chakra are usually very lonely people, though they sometimes may seem to not desire to be around others.

Keeping a gratitude journal and actively working to develop self love and compassion for others as well as being willing to forgive yourself and others are all healing activities for the heart chakra.

The **Throat Chakra** connects at the throat area in the front of the neck.

We may most easily relate to the experience of energy moving in this chakra when we are feeling tense, upset, or afraid. We get a tightness or even a lump or knot in our throat in these situations and may have a very hard time talking or even breathing well, in some cases. When you are relaxed and feel free to express yourself comfortably, you feel quite open in this area.

The Throat chakra affects the thyroid and parathyroid, the throat and voice, mouth and teeth, and the ears. It also supports our ability to express ourselves truthfully, clearly and fully, as well as being able to hear others well. This has to do with both the physical ability to communicate clearly, as well as the ability to truly give and receive the information with understanding. This chakra supports the expression of creativity as well.

When the throat chakra is not functioning well, there may be problems in the throat or voice, thyroid, mouth or teeth, ears or neck. Life issues that may occur are communication difficulties, excessive talking or fear of speaking, speaking too loudly or too softly, timidity, gossiping, lying, telling other people's secrets, being secretive and stopping the flow of creative expression.

Methods for healing this chakra include singing or chanting, listening to music and participating in creative projects.

Part 3 - Upper Chakras

The Brow, or Third Eye Chakra is located in the middle of the forehead, between the eyebrows.

We experience energy in this chakra when we feel a tightness across our forehead when we are anxious, trying to concentrate or remember something. Some may also notice a feeling of openness, tingling, coolness or other sensations during prayer, meditation, communing with nature or devotional practices which promote insight, concentration and an understanding of oneness.

This chakra affects the brain, particularly the lower and middle brain, the pituitary gland and some functions of the central nervous system, such as the autonomic. It supports the eyes as well. The third eye chakra also supports our insight and intuition, imagination, concentration and perception, wisdom, devotion, our ability to have a good memory and also helps logic and emotion to function well together.

When it is not functioning well, we are likely to have problems with our vision, our central nervous systems, neurological problems, sleep problems (excessive sleep, insomnia or nightmares), excessive daydreams, fantasies or hallucinations, paranoia and we may be disorientated in time and/or space. We may also have headaches, migraines, sinus issues, difficulty concentrating, focusing or remembering.

Issues in the third eye may keep us from trusting and connecting with others, just as issues in the heart chakra can. Methods for healing this chakra include meditation, prayer, visual stimulation, including creating visual art or journaling.

The **Crown Chakra** is located at the top of the head, where the neck of the chakra attaches.

The funnel of the chakra opens upward and extends out above the head, out into the aura.

We experience a sense of pressure or warmth in this chakra when energy is moving through it. You may have felt this during a moment of inspiration.

This chakra affects the upper part of the brain, the central nervous system and the pineal gland. It also supports our spiritual connection to the Divine, a sense that our individual self is working in unison with a Higher Self. This offers unity, purpose, service and inspiration. It allows us to have an open mind that is able to ask questions, assimilating new knowledge into intelligence.

Issues in this chakra can lead to headaches, depression, being overly religious or having a complete apathy in regard to spiritual matters, being overbearing, learning difficulty or being extremely egoic about the intellect, materialism and closed mindedness. Using your mental abilities, particularly in a new way, can be healing for this chakra, as can exposing yourself to beauty through art or nature. Learn something new. Try out new beliefs.

The Aura

The aura is the part of our energy body that extends outside of the actual physical body. In science this is called the biofield. Even non-living objects can be observed as having an aura, especially the etheric layer. The aura is often thought of in terms of being a shield, but it is much more than that. It is an energy field that exchanges and processes communication signals, just as all energy fields do. It helps us make sense of the world around us and also helps to relay information into the physical body.

The aura is essentially a blueprint or overlay of the physical body, which contains all the energetic codes needed for the body to function properly on every level, including the physical. The aura doesn't simply extend around us, but it also flows through us, integrating information into our bodies. The aura is usually referred to as having several layers or parts, which is true, but these don't neatly stack on top of each other most of the time. Rather they shift and interact with each other in a fluid way, while essentially maintaining their position. You could think of it somewhat like the rainbow rings of color you may have seen in water that has oil in it. The rings shift as the water moves, but they essentially stay in their own place.

The main layers of the aura are the etheric layer, the emotional, the mental, the astral, the etheric template, the celestial, and the causal. The etheric layer is the basic life force indicator and is the one that is the easiest for most people to see and most anyone can visualize this layer with a few minutes of practice. If you hold your hand up in front of a white wall, spread your fingers apart and let your gaze soften as you focus between the fingers to the wall behind your hand, you will see it within a minute or so.

The emotional, mental and astral layers are the ones that we often sense or that we see colors in relation to. These have to do with our thoughts and emotions, as well as our feelings of love (or the opposite) and connection to others and the world around us. If you are very empathic or sensitive, you may also sense and feel things in another's etheric template layer, picking up illnesses or impending illnesses. The celestial and causal are not as readily seen or felt as the others. These are the layers that connect us to the spiritual realms and shield us from negative aspects of the material realms.

Sometimes we read about using our auras as a shield or a bubble or protection. A healthy and well-functioning aura does much more than simply act as a bubble around our bodies. It does us a great deal of good to use our imagination to strengthen and work with our energy bodies. This is called **imaginal healing** and it is very effective as we are sending energy signals to our bodies, our brains and our cells, via our imaginations when we do this. However, we need to make full use of our imagination, fully envisioning what we wish to create in order to get the most out of the process.

To do this with the aura, straighten the spine and imagine the line of energy running up the front of the body, from the base of the pelvis to the roof of the mouth. Next, imagine the energy line running from the base of the spine to the top of the head, and connecting to the one in the front, at the roof of the mouth. In your imagination, connect these lines as a full and complete circuit of energy which flows easily in each direction, front to back and back to front, in a loop. Now imagine energy flowing out of the top of your head from this center line, pouring like a fountain of energy all around your body, 360 degrees in a toroidal field which connects at your feet and re-enters your body, flowing back up the center line of energy to begin again. If you feel any place where the energy doesn't seem to flow strongly, then focus your attention on this area for a few moments until the energy flows easily. This creates a strong and smoothly flowing energy field through your aura and into your entire system. You will feel refreshed, connected and sovereign within your own energy field.

Chapter 4 – Energy Cleansing, Grounding and Protection

Energy Cleansing, Grounding and Protection

Grounding is important to do before starting and after you finish a healing session. You will likely need to remind yourself to ground several times during the course of a healing session, particularly if you tend to be sensitive to other people's energy. We are electro-magnetic beings and we need to intentionally connect to the Earth. This helps us to both draw energy up and to release excesses of energy that have built up. In essence, it continues the circuit so that there is no overload nor an energy drainage.

You can ground in several ways, but the easiest and fastest is probably to **envision energetic tree roots** coming down your legs from your pelvis and hips, through the bottoms of your feet and deep into the core of the Earth. Imagine them flowing with energy between you and the Earth, enriching you and releasing anything that may be too much for your system.

Cleansing our energy field's is also very important before and after a session, as well as any other time we have picked up other people's energy. This is good energetic hygiene to do at the beginning and end of each day. The simplest way to do this is to perform "dry bathing." In Japanese, this process is called **Kenyoku**.

To do **Kenyoku**, or **"dry bathing"**, perform each sweep of the hands listed below on an out breath, as if you are both sweeping and blowing away stagnant or unclean energies from your energy field.

1.   Breathe in and bring your hands up to the prayer, or Gassho, position. Breathe out as you lower them to your heart center.

2.   Sweep your right hand from your left shoulder, down and across to your right hip as you breathe out.

3.   Sweep your left hand from your right shoulder, down and across to your left hip as you breathe out.

4.   Again, sweep your right hand from your left shoulder, down and across to your right hip, as you breathe out.

5.   Hold your left arm next to your side, elbow close to you. Sweep your right arm down your extended left arm from

shoulder to fingertips as you breathe out, flinging any negative energy off of the right hand as you reach the end of the left fingertips.

6.   Hold the right arm next to your side, elbow close to you. Sweep your left arm down your extended right arm from shoulder to fingertips as you breathe out, flinging the negative energy off of the left hand as you reach the end of the right fingertips.

7.   Repeat the process on the left arm once more.

8.   Breathe in and bring your hands back to the prayer, or Gassho, position. Breathe out as you lower them to your heart center. You have finished the Kenyoku technique.

Grounding and clearing your energy before and after a session will be enough for most people, but some people are highly sensitive to other people's energy, easily sensing and sometimes registering their emotions and illnesses in their own bodies. If this is the case with you, you may find that you feel most comfortable if you also add a technique such as visualizing a **sphere of gold, silver or white light** encompassing you after you finish the Kenyoku technique. Any color that feels soothing and comforting to you is what is appropriate for you.

Repeated grounding practice is very useful for highly sensitive or empathic people. Many find they benefit from salt water baths or the use of certain crystals or stones, as well. Find what works best for you to feel comfortable. It doesn't matter what works or doesn't work for others.

Grounding

Grounding is an important and often overlooked topic in our health. Grounding is simply reconnecting or realigning ourselves with the Earth or the ground. We are electrical beings with electrical currents running through our brains, nervous systems and bodies. It helps us to allow this electrical energy to ground.

There are a couple of really important reasons for grounding. First of all, the Earth has a steady supply of energy which we would naturally draw upon. Without it, we can feel drained, tired and even depressed. Secondly, we build up excess energy as we go about living our lives, through the charge of emotional energy, interactions with others and interactions with electrical equipment, for example. This can cause a feeling of overwhelm and anxiety, headaches, muscle pain or nausea. Some people have so much build up that they shock themselves or others when they touch things. This excess energy can easily be discharged and bled off into the ground through our feet without causing a disturbance and we will feel a great relief and improved well being.

It is especially important to ground before, during and after doing a Reiki treatment on a client. You will be opening your energy field to the energy field of the client, as well as to the energy of Reiki and for some people this takes their awareness out of their own body and brings more awareness of the client's issues and pain. Grounding can help keep you in your own body awareness, without taking on the issues of your client.

There are several ways to ground, so simply choose the method that feels most natural for you. Over time, it will become so natural that all you will have to do is think the word 'ground' and you will feel the magnetizing sensation in the bottoms of your feet, rooting you to the Earth as the sensation washes over your body and mind.

1.   Envision strong roots growing from the bottoms of your feet, growing down into the Earth's core.

2.   Walk outside, taking in the fresh air for a few minutes. That can be all it takes. If you feel really in need, take off your shoes and walk barefoot on the dirt or the grass.

3.   Trees are very grounding. Sit under a tree, stand with your back against one, place your palms on one, or even go all out and hug one!

4.   Play in the dirt or sand. Seriously. Play is grounding. So is gardening and being around any living thing that grows in the soil.

5.   Dance.

6.   Imagine a ball of light that begins either in your head, heart or belly. See the light drop down the center of your body, along your spine, then down your legs and out the bottoms of your feet into the Earth, connecting you to the light in the Earth.

7.   Drink a glass of water or eat something. These things activate your body, so they help to ground you.

It can be helpful to ground yourself several times a day, especially after something very draining or before and after events where you are around large numbers of other people.

Grounding Meditation

This is a basic grounding meditation that works with imagery and the basic elements of nature. It only takes about 2-3 minutes to do and it can be used anytime. When you are finished you will feel cleansed, grounded and protected. It is helpful to do this meditation as you start your day in the morning, prior to and after a healing session, and at the end of the day before you go to sleep.

It is also useful to assist in your own self-healing, particularly aiding you in releasing difficult emotions or trauma. Give it a try after an argument where your emotional buttons have been pushed or when you feel difficult memories surfacing to be healed. The lovely thing about this meditation is that it is fairly easy to use most anywhere and the more often you use it, the easier it is to visualize the imagery and call the scene to mind. The meditation will become very personalized over time as you use it, if you allow your mind to create the ideal image for you.

Start in whatever position you feel comfortable in: standing, sitting, lying down. No need to make it complicated. Simply be at ease in your body. Close your eyes. Begin to notice your breath as it moves in and out of your body. No need to alter it. Observe your breath in its normal rhythm for a few cycles, simply allowing your attention to lightly rest on your breath.

Now, imagine you are on the shore of a lovely body of crystal clear water. It is the most sparkling clean and pure water you have ever seen. Golden warm sunlight beams down onto the surface creating diamond-like glittery twinkles on the surface that remind you of the stars in the sky at night. The water looks so warm and inviting.

Let your attention begin to float through your body, doing a gentle body scan. Notice any sensations present in your body, without judging, clinging or pushing the sensation away. Maybe there is tingling, warmth or pain or something else. Whatever is there is fine. Also notice any emotions or thoughts that are present, as well as any excesses of energy that may be in your body. You may also notice things such as trauma that is stored in areas of the body. Now allow anything that you noticed to become a solid as you scan again, visualizing it on the surface of the body as dirt, mud or debris such as dried leaves or twigs that cling to your skin or hair.

Now begin to slowly walk into the warm and inviting water in front of you. As you walk into the water, feel the delicious warmth of the water caressing your skin. Notice that as it embraces your body, the debris instantly dissolves away, disappearing completely into the crystal clear water as if it had never existed. You feel lighter and lighter as you walk further into the water. Now the water is covering your lower legs. You walk deeper and it gently hugs your thighs, then your hips and belly. You are so grateful to the water for this gift.

The water continues to lovingly wash away the dirt, mud and debris from your body, pulling away all the energetic blockages and excesses that these things represented. These things are completely dissolved and renewed in the water. As you walk deeper, your chest and neck are now gently embraced by the warm water. Lastly, your head is able to feel the loving energy of the water as it pours over your crown. This water is comforting, you are perfectly able to breathe and you feel safe. Continue walking, allowing the water to wash away and dissolve mud and debris from your system. Walk to the other side and begin to ascend the incline back out of the body of water.

As you walk out of the water, notice how the water is pulled off of you by Earth's gravitational pull. Allow the force of the water being pulled off of you to drain off any remaining debris, if you still notice any at all. Tune in to the water draining around your legs and your lower pelvis, between your legs. Earth's gravity is pulling the water very hard. Allow your own energy to connect with the Earth's pull so that you can also connect through your root chakra to the Earth. Feel the sensation of it pulling you down. Give your gratitude to the Earth for your connection to the ground.

Now notice a soft and warm wind creating a gentle vortex around you, drying the rest of the water and cleansing you further. Imagine the element of air giving you a soft embrace. Notice that the warm rays of the sun seem to have focused their warmth directly on your head and shoulders. You feel a gentle warming and pulsing sensation entering your body at the top as your root and feet pull you down. The sensation surrounds and fills you softly, like a whisper. Next, a beam of blue heavenly light directs itself into your crown chakra, filling you with protective energy. This energy flows down your body, filling you with peace, comfort and gentle confidence. Give your deep thanks as well to the wind, the sun and the Divine for their assistance in this meditation.

Dark or Stuck Energy, Cords and "Entities"

When you hear about dark or stuck energy, does it make you uncomfortable? What about cord cutting? When I first began doing energy work, these things made me uneasy. I had sensed these things in others energy fields for years, but didn't know what they meant or what to do about them. As I learned more, they became less frightening.

Dark or stuck energy often appears as a thick brown or black cloud in the aura or body of a person. It is simply an area where not enough energy or life force (light) is flowing through. These can often be seen by sensitive people in other places as well, such as houses or other buildings and most objects that people and living beings have been active around for any length of time.

Dark, stuck energy is not a scary as it may sound. It is simply an energy that didn't flow through. It got caught and became stagnant. It may have been a very difficult emotion that the person was unable to process fully that got stuck in a repetitive loop of thought-emotion-thought. These can become lodged in the tissues and cause illness, which will appear as darkness.

Negative emotions are very constrictive in nature. When they are experienced and then released, there is usually no blockage and energy resumes its normal flow. But when there are repeated negative emotions, or when thought patterns become such that the person remains stuck in processing the old emotional pattern, the emotional energy can't flow through and release. The pathway remains constricted and becomes blocked.

We can become caught in patterns of thought or in relational patterns that are destructive or that once served to keep us healthy or safe, but are no longer needed. If we continue to operate out of these old patterns due to fear or habit, they can generate stuck and dense energy as well. These dark energies get stuck in our energy field and lock in the pattern, keeping us stuck there and making it harder to break free and often making it difficult to even recognize we are stuck.

These dark densities can sometimes seem to take on a life of their own, which is when they begin to be referred to as entities. This is when we have given an energy power over us for so long that it has its own strength. We empower many emotions and thought forms in this way. Those who are involved in highly charged and unhealthy thought patterns may be unwittingly empowering entities in their energy field and the environment around them. These entities are mainly made of and fed on emotional energy and the negative emotional energy that charges these individuals and family situations is what keep them alive. When the situation is healed, they have nothing to live on, so they leave.

This sounds a bit frightening, but the truth is nearly everyone has some degree of entities around them and in their field. We are all working toward the light. While these entities can become very controlling and nasty in some cases, that is not usually what happens. If this does happen, you may need special assistance to remove the entity, such as a shaman who works with entity removal. However, healing the original cause is highly important.

When densities appear, the channels can be opened back up so that the energy (light) can move again. Reiki or other energy work is helpful to do this. It is also helpful to remove the dark or dense energy blockage. Reiki will reduce the size of a blockage on its own and most practitioners are able to see or feel a blockage and energetically "pull" it out. This may take more than one session for larger densities.

Cord cutting brings to mind the idea of something painful. Or the thought that you will be removing yourself from someone or something that you don't wish to be separated from. There is no physical cutting involved in the process. It is all energetic. It is actually the cutting away of unhealthy emotional energy that is stuck in a loop and can't release. It keeps the person stuck and unable to break loose or think clearly for themselves.

These cords can be found and cut with energy. The area is then healed so that a new cord is less likely to grow back and also to soothe the pain of the release. This does not end relationships. It may help soothe the pain of old tethers to a relationship that is already over and ended, but it will not end a healthy relationship. It may also end unhealthy attachments in an otherwise loving relationship, so that it may flourish.

When you actively and honestly engage yourself in your own healing process, there is little to fear in the darkness. The healing process will not always be a pleasant or easy one, but if you commit yourself to it, the darkness will always come to light.

Cord Removal and Clearing

Cord cutting, cord dissolving, cord clearing, cord removal and removal of attachments are all terms that represent the same general things. These terms seem to evoke a lot of emotion in people, of one extreme or another. There is a great deal of misunderstanding about what cords and attachments are and what their removal entails and what the result of that will be.

Cords are the emotional energy that exists between two people in any relationship, whether it is a family relationship, a work relationship, a friendship or an intimate relationship. They are nothing to fear. We all have them and they are normal. Our systems are always sending out energy and receiving energy from our environment and from the other energy beings around us.

When we interact directly with someone, we send out cords of energy vibrations that send and receive energy signals, which facilitate our communications. To those who can see them, they appear as wavy, flowing energy lines that connect the parties who are interacting. Even if no words are being said, when two people are involved in a relationship of some type or have strong emotional energy toward each other, these cords can be seen or felt by those sensitive to this. Again, this is normal and it is happening constantly, just as your eyes are constantly seeing, your ears are constantly hearing and your skin is constantly sensing.

When we are in ongoing relationships, we often develop a build-up of certain emotional energies in our tissues and in our mental and emotional bodies. Even in a healthy relationship, we have periods where there is a lot of negative emotional energy or it is simply a difficult time. This can also happen after a loss or a death. In difficult, abusive or co-dependent relationships, there will be much negative energy build-up and many difficult periods to release. When we are ready to let go of the energy of that and release those periods of our relationship, we can do a cord cutting to facilitate the process.

Cord cutting can also ease the process if we are ready to let go of a relationship or if a relationship is ending naturally. Cord cutting **will not** and cannot end a relationship that isn't already ending naturally or that you or the other partly are not ready to end. That is not the purpose of cord cutting. It does not interfere in any way with the outcome of the relationship. That is solely between you and the other person and any decisions each of you choose to make. Cord cutting is simply a tool to help remove, dissolve and heal an old, damaging emotional energy that has become attached to you from the relationship. This helps you heal and it does often help the relationship move in new directions. Sometimes these directions are with the two of you moving closer together in a more healed way (which is what everyone wants, of course!) and other times it is the two of you finding resolution apart. Ultimately, cord cutting is about releasing the past and the ways it has attached itself to you and formed harmful patterns in your cells and in your habits so that you can find peace and move forward in a new way. Remaining open to what that new way might be helps you to be fully open to your healing process.

Cord cutting is done by scanning as you do a Reiki session and locating areas that feel dense, hot or cold. When you find these areas, ensure that you are fully grounded and your aura is strong, and then imagine a small violet flame next to you. This is a helpful and healing, yet strong energy that can handle the cord and the density that you are going to pull out of the person. Lifting your hand slightly above the body, in the aura above the area where you feel the density, heat or cold of the cord attachment, begin to *"pull"* the dense energy out. If you feel resistance, slow down and ask the Higher Self of the client to release it. That is usually enough for it to break free. See it dissolving from their cells and aura and imagine any holes or weakness in their aura sealing back up and the cord density leaves. Place the density into the violet flame that you envisioned earlier. Finish by placing your hands over the area and sending Reiki for as long as feels appropriate. Use all of the symbols over the area to strengthen and seal it.

An alternative method for doing this is to us a cutting or chopping motion with the hand as you blow out sharply. This feels more aggressive to me and I prefer the gentler method I described above, which is at least as effective, if not more so. I do sometimes use the breath, as I feel guided to do so.

You may not feel much the first few times you do this, and you may question whether you are imagining most of it. Trust what you feel. It's real and after the session when you speak to the client you will find verification, if you need it.

Reiki Housecleaning

Most of us don't really enjoy cleaning our house, but you can infuse Reiki into the process and feel a real lift as you go through. It will pick you up and also make your whole house feel lighter and more energetically free.

Here are a few simple suggestions taken from my own housecleaning routine. Put on some music that makes you feel calm, yet motivated and try these out the next time you clean. I expect you'll feel better about the process and I'm sure your home will feel very peaceful when you are done.

1. Start your housecleaning session by smudging your house. You may not feel you need to do this every time, depending on how many people live in your home and how many visitors you have. I do a big housecleaning once a week and I smudge each time. It is also a good idea to do this with any major cleaning, such as spring cleaning or when you clean out a room or a closet, as this will clear out any stale, heavy energies that have been lodged in those areas with old belongings. Set your new intentions for your home and seal it with Reiki in the walls and doors.

2. Send Reiki to your cleaning tools as you go. As you progress, take a moment to send Reiki to your vacuum, your broom and mop, your cleaning products. Each time you do this, you will feel refreshed as well and you will notice that the task you are performing seems lighter. This is one way that I enact the Reiki precept of **"Just for today, I will do my work diligently and honestly"**. Allow the energy of Reiki to flow directly through you into the tools for the task, for the greatest good. Allow it to help you see greater ways to love your home and allow it to support you. Allow it to help you see greater ways to give and receive love to those you share your home with, uplifting all of you.

3. Infuse the beds with Reiki as you make them. This helps with peaceful sleep and prevents disturbing dreams.

4. Infuse your pet's food and water when you clean their bowls. This helps to boost the health benefits of the food and water and allows your pet to receive a boost of Reiki as they eat and drink. It balances the energy of the food and water, just as it does when you send Reiki to your own food and water.

5. Send Reiki to your plants when you water them and to their water, as well. Plants benefit from Reiki as much as any living thing! You will feel the pull of energy as they soak it up.

6. As you dust, send a Reiki blessing to the items and appliances you clean. This is as simple as shifting your state of mind to one of gratitude and allowing Reiki to flow from your eyes and hands as you dust. Be grateful for the computer, the TV, the refrigerator and all the food in it, the bookshelf and all the wonderful books it holds, for all the lovely items your home contains for you and for all the people you love who use them. Love them deeply. **"Just for today I will be filled with gratitude".** Allow this energy to pour from you.

7. Any time you use water, bless it with Reiki. Whether you are doing dishes, cleaning the bathroom or taking a break to have a glass of water, make a point of saying 'thank you' and offering a brief blessing of Reiki to the water as it flows. We are so fortunate to have clean water running directly from our taps and we often take that privilege for granted. The tasks you perform would be much more difficult without it, so thank the water and bless it. Have gratitude for the bathroom itself and for the sink in which you can wash your dishes. Be especially grateful for the refreshing glass of water which you drink.

As you go through you housecleaning infusing everything with Reiki and bringing to mind the Reiki principles, you may still not enjoy cleaning your house--though you might! -- but you will feel better and lighter. You can't help but feel good when you are doing Reiki and the principles will shift your state of mind to a freer place. It is a myth that you have to dread cleaning! Sweep that myth away with the dust!

Purification and Cleansing Spray

Clearing and purifying your home, your healing space and your aura regularly is an energetic necessity for maintaining your well-being. This is especially true when you are working with others on a regular basis or if you are highly sensitive or empathic. Burning sage or incense is one of the most popular methods of quickly and effectively clearing old, stagnant or negative energy and had been my preferred method until recently. Then I began developing a dislike for the smell of burning sage and soon after that, my sinuses and lungs would become irritated after I saged the house. My body needed me to find another method of quickly clearing energy.

There are many tools that the Earth offers us to help clear energy and different ways that we can use them. Burning flowers, leaves and essences or oils (as in incense) makes use of the fire element to release the purifying energy in the flowers, leaves or oils and this is very effective as the smoke carries the energy to many regions, cleansing as it goes. Fire is also very cleansing, so making use of this element to ignite the flowers, leaves or oils is beneficial.

However, we can make use of other elements to cleanse our auras and our homes. Water is a very useful element for cleansing, and we use it every time we bathe, shower or clean our home. To make use of the water element as an intentional purification and clearing spray, we need to prepare in advance by adding the other Earth elements we wish to use to offer cleansing and purification. Always use purified or distilled water, since you only want to add the purest possible energy for this purpose. Adding sea salt boosts the purifying effects, since sea salt is very cleansing and is also grounding. You can be creative in choosing herbs, flowers, flower essences and essential oils that you feel intuitively guided to or attracted to. There are many that have the properties of anointing, purification or cleansing.

I like to add Bach's Rescue Remedy to my Purification Spray. It is a flower essence and it has an overall uplifting, cleansing and healing effect. I also like to add up to 6 drops of essential oils. Lemon oil, frankincense, lavender, rose, clary sage, patchouli, jasmine, tea tree and cedar wood oil are all good options. You can also choose a blend that has some of these in it. Dry or fresh herbs such as sage, thyme, rosemary and basil are all useful. The leaves, flowers and stem of the lavender is useful to add, as is dried lavender. You may add dried rose petals or other dried or fresh flower petals, as flower energy is always uplifting and dispels negative energy. (It is useful to keep a bouquet of flowers and some potted plants and herbs to generally uplift the energy in your home!)

The recipe below can be used as spray to cleanse your aura or to purify and cleanse your home or healing space. You can also use it to cleanse your crystals after use in a healing session. I now use this in place of burning sage or a smudge stick.

Purification and Cleansing Spray:

2, 4 ounce glass or metal spray bottles
8 ounces of very warm, but not hot purified or distilled water
1 Tablespoon alcohol (unflavored vodka) or witch hazel, to preserve
1 Tablespoon sea salt
1 Tablespoon dried rosemary or 1 sprig of fresh rosemary
1 Tablespoon dried sage leaf or 2-3 fresh sage leaves

Pinch of dried basil or 1-2 fresh basil leaves

1 teaspoon dried lavender or small spring of fresh lavender

1 teaspoon dried rose petals

4 drops essential oils

3 droppers of Rescue Remedy (optional)

3 cloves

◊ Steep all ingredients in the warm, distilled or purified water for 20 minutes. Stir.

◊ Line a sieve with a piece of cheesecloth or a paper towel and place it over a bowl. Pour the mixture through to strain and let it drain into the bowl.

◊ Pour into the spray bottles and place the lids on them. Label them.

◊ If you like, place several crystals around the bottles for a few hours so that the spray becomes charged with the added energy of the crystals. Make sure to give Reiki for to your spray for a few minutes, as well!

◊ Shake well before using each time.

Spray into your aura, all around your body to cleanse the aura. Spray around your home or healing space to clear negative energy, making sure to spray corners, closets and doorways, and areas of particular density or negativity. Any area where there is a lot of traffic or lots of electronic equipment use should be sprayed often. Do not spray directly on electronic equipment! You will probably use this spray frequently, but make sure to use it all within about a month. It is all natural and everything natural eventually begins to decompose and turn stale.

Remember, you can also use Reiki to cleanse your aura and any space, alone or with another method.

Smudging to Cleanse Energy

Smudging is an ancient technique used by many cultures to purify and bless the energy of people and their spaces. In the West, it is most often associated with the many Native America tribes, but many cultures around the world have the custom of burning herbs or incense for these same purposes. Many places of worship use some variation of this before or during their rituals or services.

Typically, sage is the herb that is used for smudging. There are many varieties of sage and any can be used, though white sage is the most common. Sage smoke is very effective for clearing and removing negative energy. Cedar or sweetgrass or other herbs, such as lavender can also be used to smudge, although these herbs are generally better used to infuse positive energy and are not as effective as sage at removing negative energy. They can be useful to burn after smudging with sage, or can be bundled into a smudge wand along with sage to be burned at the same time.

Smudging is an excellent practice to do regularly for yourself and in your home as basic energetic hygiene. It is very useful to do after you have guests in order to clear the home of the energy of those that do not live there and any issues they may have brought in with them. It is also good to do during and after an illness or an argument to cleanse the home of the negative energy around these issues. If you move, smudging is a very useful way to clear your new home of the energy of the former residents, leaving a clean slate for you and your family.

If you want to smudge yourself or your home, you can buy a smudge stick, which is dried sage leaves bundled together, or you can simply buy loose sage leaves. Have a ceramic or clay bowl nearby before you start. This is to lay the smudge stick in after you light it and can also be used to safely extinguish it after you are finished.

I put a layer of sea salt in the bottom of my clay bowl. It serves as an addition aid in purification, I know that it won't burn, and I can extinguish the sage in it safely without getting the entire stick wet. I usually use loose sage leaves, laying two or three directly on top of the bed of sea salt in my clay bowl. Sage leaves can be left to burn out on their own but it's best to put a wand out when you're done. Put it out by snuffing it in the salt bed in your bowl, rubbing it out, or wetting it.

Open a window in each room, at least a crack before you start. This encourages the smoke to leave the house, carrying any negative energy with it. Besides, you don't want a heavy build up of smoke in your house! Set your intention to cleanse your space and call upon your guides. Call upon north, south, east, west, above, below and within.

Then you can light the end of you smudge stick (the leafy end, not the stemmy, woody end) or the few sage leaves in your clay bowl. Once they are burning well, gently blow the fire out. If you are using a smudge stick, lay it down in the bowl. Rub your hands together in the smoke, just as you would if you were washing them, allowing the smoke to wash the energy of your hands. Then use your hands to direct and "pour" the smoke over your head, directing it across the top of your head, your eyes, ears, mouth and throat. Intend that the smoke clear you so that you can think, see, hear and speak clearly and peacefully, with love. Continue using your hands to direct smoke to your heart, solar plexus and lower belly. Then carefully pick up the bowl and run the smoke under each of your feet. You will quickly feel the shift in your energy, feeling lighter and more peaceful.

You can smudge another person by directing the smoke toward their body, using your hand or a feather. Start at their feet and work your way up, focusing on the chakra areas and hands and any areas of density you observe or sense in the aura.

To smudge your home, after smudging yourself, start at the front entrance of the main room of the home and move around the home in a counterclockwise direction (work to your left) Direct the smoke or let the smoke pass into all areas, especially around the perimeter and in corners. To be very thorough, open cabinets and closets and allow the smoke to waft into them as well. When you have completed the smudge and come back to the front entrance, take any ashes you have outside and place them on the earth to discard them.

If you like, you can burn a candle (beeswax candles are great!) or a sprig of lavender to seal in positive energy after cleansing your home through smudging.

How to Make an Energy Ball with Reiki

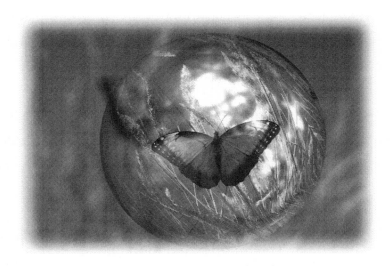

Energy balls are also called chi balls and some people call them Reiki balls when using them with Reiki energy. I have found energy balls to be very useful in combination with Reiki. They can be used to help send an energy boost at a distance, to charge a room with long term Reiki, slowly releasing Reiki energy, or to "*hold*" slow releasing energy for a specific person or issue until the right time for it to release, for the greater good.

Broadly speaking, an energy ball is a mass of electro magnetically charged energy that is filled with an intention. That sounds pretty high tech, but really it just means you are rolling a ball of energy in between your hands and sending thought and intention into the ball. It is very simple. We send the intentions for Reiki to be activated into the ball, much as we would have those intentions when we are doing distant Reiki or even when working in person with a client.

Bring to mind the intention for which you are making the ball. For example, if you are making an energy ball to send to a future appointment for a stressed loved one, then intend healing for the highest good in that situation.

To start the ball, hold your hands close together, palm to palm. Ask Reiki to flow and begin to feel the energy. Rub your hands together for a second or two, if this feels right to you. Move your hands about an inch apart and notice the pull of energy between them. Now move them closer together and notice the pushing sensation. Much of that is your own energy field. You may also be feeling warmth and tingling or pulsing sensations as the Reiki flows through your hands. A few practitioners don't notice these sensations, especially at first or if they don't practice regularly. Don't worry if you don't feel it. Nothing is wrong and the Reiki energy ball will still work! Like all things, Reiki takes practice and working with it, so practice this and you will soon notice the effects of your energy balls.

Turn your hands so that one hand is on top of the other, fingertips to the opposite wrist, in front of the lower belly. Cup your hands slightly as if you are holding a ball. Notice any energy pulsing sensations and begin rotating your hands in opposite directions, as if shaping and molding a ball. The top hand will rotate in a clockwise direction and the bottom hand will rotate in a counter-clockwise direction. Think of any symbols you wish to use, choosing whichever ones might be most appropriate for the person or situation you are sending the energy healing ball to. It is not necessary to use any healing symbols at all. I have successfully used Reiki balls even while I was a Level 1 practitioner and many other times when I chose not to use symbols. If you choose to use symbols, you can simply think the symbols, draw them with your tongue on the roof of your mouth or say their name silently or aloud. They will activate with intention. Intend that any chosen symbols are now sent into the energy ball and ask that they assist it in its healing. Spend a moment sealing and blessing the healing. Give gratitude to Reiki, the Divine and your guides and angels for any assistance in this healing.

Lastly, "*push*" the energy ball into whatever you are intending to heal. If it is meant for yourself, push it into your own body. For another, push it into or toward them. For a situation, you can push it in the general direction that you believe the situation will occur in. For a room, you can push the ball into a wall, floor, ceiling or door to bless the room and ask for long term Reiki healing and protection to release as needed from the ball.

Most anything can benefit from a Reiki ball! Use your imagination and think of the ways you can ask Reiki and energy balls to assist you in your daily life!

Chapter 5 – Reiki and Healthcare

Reiki and Multiple Sclerosis

I have noticed the increase in neurological and autoimmune diseases over the last decade or so. Having suffered with seizures, migraines and various autoimmune difficulties, I am particularly interested in the treatment of these types of illness. I also have family members who have suffered with stroke and dementia. Most of us have been affected by neurological and autoimmune disorders in some way during the course of our lives. When I found that a friend's daughter had been diagnosed with Multiple Sclerosis, I began researching complementary and alternative methods for treating MS. I would like to share with you some of the information I found regarding using Reiki to treat MS.

Reiki was researched for the treatment of MS in a 2002 study in the United Kingdom. Very positive results were found. It was a small group of study participants (ten in all), with patients ranging from 35 to 60 years old. They were treated with Reiki once a week, for one hour, over the course of twelve weeks. The participants were tested on motor function, cognitive function, fatigue and lethargy, emotional and mental well-being, sensation in the arms and legs, pain, and urinary and bowel problems. All the participants saw improvement in symptoms and one person was completely relieved of all symptoms.

In particular, the participants had significant decreases in pain and depression symptoms. Some of them were still noticing the relief nine months after the treatments had stopped, while others had some return of symptoms 6-8 weeks after the sessions were stopped.

Ninety percent of the participants had a reduction of pain, eighty percent had a reduction of motor symptoms, seventy percent had a reduction of fatigue and seventy-one percent noticed a reduction of the symptoms in their legs. Other areas of improvement were a reduction of urinary symptoms (66%), a reduction in bowel symptoms (60%), a reduction in lethargy (60%), and a reduction in the symptoms in the arms (42%). All but one patient noticed a significant reduction in cognitive symptoms. That patient experienced no change in cognitive symptoms during the study. In the patients who experienced sleeplessness or dizziness, symptoms were completely relieved during the 12-week study. Those with stomach pains had a reduction of symptoms.

In another case I found during my research, a woman with MS was unable to walk. She began using Reiki and reflexology. After a year, she is completely relieved of symptoms and can walk again. She described her symptoms in this way "elastic bands of pain circling my body, weak heavy legs, impaired walking, no mobility upon rising, dropping things, blurred or double vision, severe mood swings, poor or no bladder control, back pain and swelling, impaired speech, pins and needle sensation throughout my body, and my symptoms were aggravated by heat."

I find all of this very encouraging. In many cases, patients with MS are not helped by traditional medicine alone. Even in the best of cases, traditional medicine only tries to delay the onset and worsening of symptoms. Cures and total relief of symptoms are rare with MS. Combining Reiki treatments with traditional medicine seems to have enormous benefits to MS patients.

Several studies have confirmed that Reiki reduces depression, anxiety and pain symptoms. Even if these were the only symptoms relieved with Reiki, this would be a tremendous help to MS sufferers. Pain, depression and anxiety are believed to worsen the condition of the immune system and the ability to cope. When these things are improved, a person is better able to heal. Reiki can be a very important tool in the treatment of Multiple Sclerosis, relieving a number of symptoms and lessening the distress associated with the illness.

Links to discussions of the research sites:

----

http://www.therapeuticreiki.com/blog/reiki-ms/,

http://www.thehealingpages.com/research-into-reiki-and-multiple-sclerosis

Reiki and Mental Health

In my recent research on the effects of Reiki on various illnesses, I came across studies that found Reiki to be very beneficial for the treatment of depression and anxiety. I found this very encouraging and wanted to look into Reiki and mental health more deeply. What I found was that scientific studies in this area are limited at this time. However, based on what has been studied and what is known about Reiki, it does seem that Reiki can be an effective therapy in the treatment of mental illness.

In one study of Reiki and depression, patients were given Reiki for six weeks for an hour to an hour and a half each time. In this study, there was a control group that did not receive Reiki treatments at all. The patients that received Reiki had a significant improvement in depression and stress symptoms as compared to the control group, which had almost no change at all. A year later, the study participants reported continued relief. Other studies measured the effects of Reiki on anxiety and found very similar results to those in the depression study. Another study included patients with a diagnosis of Post Traumatic Stress Disorder (PTSD) and found that the participants found great relief of symptoms from this as well.

There are studies that examine the effect of various complementary and alternative therapies on schizophrenia. These studies looked at the general effect of meditation, yoga, massage and other therapies like Reiki, according to which a participant chose to use. The effects of these types of therapies (including Reiki) were that the patients saw a large improvement in their level of coping and sense of well being.

In an interesting real world example, a group of mental health patients met with a Reiki master and several practitioners to receive Reiki once a week. They had all been recently released from hospital treatment and participated in a daily routine of outpatient groups. The patients had diagnoses of severe depression, schizophrenia, drug and alcohol addiction and other mental disabilities. The Reiki master that led the group of treatments said that many times the third eye and throat chakras were incredibly open while the heart chakra was generally closed. She saw a lot of improvement in the patients she treated and many asked to be attuned to Reiki so they could continue to help themselves.

Many studies have been done that demonstrate that Reiki regulates the pulse rate, blood pressure and immune system. This shows that Reiki produces a tremendous level of peace, calm and relaxation, which can only help those with mental health problems, regardless of what the diagnosis may be. It is well known that increasing relaxation increases a person's state of overall wellness and encourages healing on all levels.

With regard to mental illness, we have to take in more than the physical aspect to include the mental, emotional and spiritual aspect of the patient. When a person's chakras are unbalanced, then imbalance ensues on all levels. One way this can manifest is through mental and emotional disturbance, inability to process incoming information, hallucinations and delusions. While there are no scientific studies to validate it, we know that Reiki balances the chakras. Balancing the chakras and promoting the relaxation response may provide a great deal of help to provide relief from the symptoms of mental illness and provide comfort to a patient as they heal.

I am certain that there will be further studies into Reiki and mental health as the effectiveness of Reiki on other health conditions is proven. In the meantime, we know Reiki can do no harm and often does a great deal of good. Given that knowledge and the studies we already have, it seems that offering Reiki to the mentally ill can only have positive results.

Reiki and Epilepsy

Since I began on my path with Reiki, I have become very interested in learning about its benefits for neurological disorders. I suffered with different types of epileptic seizures and the related issues for 20 years and noticed that once I was attuned to Reiki and practicing daily self-Reiki, the neurological issues reduced significantly. I went from having migraines and twitching every day to very rarely having these issues at all. Now if I get a migraine, it's mild instead of debilitating. I have only had one seizure-like episode in 6 years. At one time, I was having some type of seizure nearly every day and even at my best, I rarely went more than a year or so without an episode.

In researching Reiki and epilepsy, I found that a great many people with epilepsy have tried Reiki and found that their seizures were either greatly reduced or stopped completely after having treatments. There are reports from adults as well as from parents of children who say that they obtained relief from large numbers of seizures after a series of Reiki treatments. Most of them had a series of treatments, usually over the course of a few months.

I also found reports from Reiki practitioners who have had results using Reiki on epilepsy sufferers. I found it interesting that a common suggestion among Reiki practitioners who use this to treat epilepsy is to treat the feet first, instead of the head. This is the same suggestion that I noticed when researching using Reiki with those who suffer from anxiety, depression or other mental health disorders. In fact, it seems that in treating any issue where the patient may tend to be ungrounded or have an excess of activity in the head, it is often suggested to start in the feet and work up, rather than the traditional method. I do recognize that starting at the Earth Star and Root chakra often works best for me personally, during my Reiki self-healing, as my head area often feels too active at the beginning of a treatment and I can't settle in as well. The energy can feel too much in that area until I have calmed my energy down and grounded.

I found one scientific research study that used a Reiki type healing method and meditation to test 15 patients with epilepsy against a control group. These patients had refractory seizures, which means that their seizures were could no longer be controlled by any medications, despite the fact that they were taking them properly. None of the patients had any other major health issues. After undergoing 3 months of Reiki type hands on healing and daily meditation, they all showed a significant reduction in seizures. The researchers concluded that further studies were warranted in this area.

Based on this research, both scientific and experiential, it seems that Reiki does help with epilepsy for a large number of people. Personally, I find that I benefit from having a Reiki session or two from someone else now and then, in addition to my daily self-Reiki. I also notice that I have more issues when I skip days with self-Reiki, so I have learned not to do that.

I will continue to look into the ways Reiki can benefit neurological conditions. As I find out more, I will share it.

----

[1] http://www.neurologyindia.com/article.asp?issn=0028-3886;year=2003;volume=51;issue=2;spage=211;epage=214;aulast=Kumar

Chapter 6 – Reiki Tips

Meditation and Reiki

I was already a meditator when I decided to take my first Reiki class, so I knew the value of meditation in releasing unhealthy and illusory thought patterns and opening the mind to a more expansive and clear way of understanding things. The day of my first class, I came home and sat in meditation observing the new ways that energy moved through me after the Reiki attunement and the enhanced way I could sense and see energy around me. It was my first meditation on Reiki energy and it was the beginning of an important journey on my Reiki path.

I have come to see that mediation and Reiki are very close companions in our self-healing journey. Using Reiki as a system of hand placements for healing is wonderfully helpful and should be practiced daily. But it is also very important to spend some time each day meditating on the Reiki principles and to notice how the energy feels as it moves within us. If you are level 2 or above, it is important that you spend some time meditating on the symbols, as well.

Meditating on the principles, the Reiki energy, and the symbols starts out as a method of understanding more about Reiki, but over time you will realize it is also a way in which you learn about life and about your inner self. You come to learn more about your connection to Source or God through these practices. Ultimately, this is part of the self-healing practice of Reiki.

None of this needs to be very complicated and each person can find the method that feels the most appropriate to them. The important thing is to have some time in which you explore the ways that these things feel to you and what meaning they have in your life.

There are several methods that have worked well for me over time. By using your imagination, you will likely be able to come up with one or more that is well suited to you.

1.   **Spend a minute or so contemplating one or more of the Reiki principles at the beginning of each self-Reiki**

session. Rather than reciting the principles through rote memory, really take a moment and notice how you feel about them and what they might mean in your life. For example, what lies underneath anger or worry for you? In what way do you typically respond to these emotions, both internally and externally? You might also contemplate how the principles support each other and how they can best support you in your growth and healing.

2. **During self-Reiki, notice the way Reiki moves within you.** Contemplate the Source of Reiki energy. How do you see that? How does it feel to you today? You can also use the time while you are practicing self-Reiki to contemplate the principles, or the symbols.

3. **Set aside a specific meditation time just for Reiki contemplation.** Perhaps you can set aside a 5-10 minutes session each weekend just for focusing on one or more Reiki symbols or the principles, or some aspect of Reiki that has come into play in your life over that past week.

4. **Some of my favorite ways to contemplate and meditate on Reiki are in the shower, as I drive or as I do housework.** These activities are relaxing and meditative to my mind and I find that whatever I am mentally focused on prior to starting seems to become clearer as I am performing the task. Maybe you have a similar task or hobby that allows your mind to relax and see more clearly.

5.   **Journal about the principles.** This can also work well for contemplating the Source of Reiki. Journaling about what you discover can be very helpful. Writing is a wonderful way to help us explore our inner world and it leaves a record for us to return to later.

Please keep in mind as you do you meditation practices that there is no right or wrong way to do this. You don't have to sit on the floor cross legged—or sit at all! Go for a walk or a run, if that feels better to you. The idea is to spend some time contemplating these things and learn what they mean in your life. There is no right or wrong answer for what you will find, either. In fact, it will change over time as you learn more about yourself. Some days you may find it very challenging and it may even bring up anger or other emotions. This is all part of your own healing process, so I encourage you to continue returning to it, despite any difficulties. **The rewards are worth it.**

Using Reiki with Animals

I have been empathically connected to animals all my life. I can understand how they hurt, what they fear and what makes them happy. I have been instinctively helping animals using communication and touch since before I knew what Reiki was. Animals are beings expanding their consciousness and spirituality just as humans are. Healing animals is important as it helps not only the animal, but humans as well.

Offering Reiki to an animal is different than giving Reiki to a person. I would like to address some of the ways I have found to help animals most effectively.

1. Be calm and relaxed when approaching an animal. Animals can easily sense our state of mind. When there is fear or upset in you, the same is created in the animal.

A frightened animal is less likely to accept Reiki, and may lash out. Conversely, a state of peace and calm will soothe the animal, allowing it to more readily accept Reiki. I recommend meditating near the animal with the intent to allow Reiki to flow.

2. Animals are much more sensitive to energy than humans. Because of this, hands-on Reiki can seem like too much for them, particularly at the beginning. Always open your hands gently, at your sides or in your lap. Allow Reiki to flow from this position. This will help the animal feel more at ease with you.

3. Ask for permission to send Reiki. Animals like to feel that they are able to have some control over their lives, just as we do. Let them know that you are there to help. Tell them that you will listen to them as they guide how the Reiki session will go. If the animal is accepting, they will let you know by remaining nearby. They may become very still and may relax and go to sleep within a short period. Some animals need to continue moving around during Reiki, but they will stay nearby if they are interested in receiving. Use your intuition to guide you.

4. Let the animal guide your hands. If hands-on Reiki is something the animal feels they want, then they will move to your hands. Often they will place the body part they want treated into or near your hands. The animal knows better than anyone else where the Reiki will most help. Follow their lead. Never place your hands on an animal unless they have let you know they want you to. Just like with people, each one is different and sessions will vary, even with the same patient. Don't assume the animal wants hands-on, even if it did before.

5. Follow the animal's lead. When the animal lets you know he is done receiving Reiki, respect that, even if it's only been a few minutes. End the session and thank the animal for participating. Each animal will let you know in their own way when they are done with the session. They may simply leave, or become engaged in another activity; they may wake from their "Reiki nap" and sniff your hands. If they decide to receive hands-on Reiki, don't change hand positions if it seems that you may disturb the animal's relaxed state. Let the animal guide the session.

Both pets and wildlife enjoy Reiki and benefit from it. I often stand outside in a quiet wooded area and open my hands, offering Reiki to any that wish to receive it. The response is always amazing! Animals come out of nowhere to soak up the Reiki. Many of them stand within a few feet away and quite often fall asleep right in front of me. Birds, mammals, frogs, fish and insects such as dragonflies and butterflies have all come to close to me to receive Reiki. Healing animals contributes to healing the wounds humans have caused them over the millennia. Healing any creature heals us all. We are all one.

Reiki Boxes

One of the best ways to use Reiki on a daily basis is with a Reiki box or a Reiki list. This is an efficient way to send healing to several people and situations all at once, in a short amount of time. This makes it possible to treat quite a few people with a bit of Reiki every day over a long period, which can be very helpful for those who are chronically ill or for situations that are ongoing and will need continued treatment over a long period of time.

A Reiki box can be anything that you place the names of those people and situations to be healed into. You could use an old shoe box, a recipe file, an index card holder, or even a simple pocket folder. Use a clay jar or a bowl. You can also use the free Reiki Rays app for your phone. Use your imagination. The idea is to have one place where all of the Reiki energy can be focused each day. One place where you can focus on each name and situation as you send healing energy.

You can decorate your selected box, if you choose. You could place a crystal in or on your Reiki box, as this will amplify the healing energy. You may want to find some way to distinguish it from other items in your home, even if you choose not to decorate it. Something that designates it as a special and sacred place for healing. One thing you could choose to do is to smudge the box to cleanse its energy.

Write a list of names and situations to send Reiki to, or write each name on an individual card or strip of paper, and place it in the box. You could add any situations that trouble you from the news, or world situations that you are aware need healing. You may add the names of loved ones who are ill or going through difficulty, as long as they would consent to receiving Reiki. If you are not aware that they would be OK with receiving Reiki, you may wish to keep a separate list or box for simple prayer. Now you are ready to use it each day.

To use your Reiki box, simply focus your intention on the names and situations that you have on the list in your box and let the Reiki flow to them for several minutes. I usually do this for 3-5 minutes each day.

This really works wonders. Paths to healing and peace seem to open up, sometimes in amazing ways, where none were available before. It seems so simple and so unlikely that it would have an effect treating a list of names for just a few minutes each morning, but I see the incredible shifts that happen each time I pick the practice back up again. There is no doubt in my mind that it works. Give it a try for yourself and see!

Using Reiki with Other Healing Tools

I write frequently about the many ways to use Reiki in your everyday life. The uses are endless. There is actually nothing you can't apply intention and Reiki to. There are many other useful healing tools we can make use of throughout our day which Reiki energy can boost the effectiveness of, even if we don't use these methods in a professional Reiki practice.

Once you begin to develop your understanding of the fact that we are literally immersed in the Universal Energy that supports all life, you begin to understand that we are actually always interacting with it. It is within us and all around us. It is within and all around everything and everyone we encounter. Recognizing this allows us to begin to interact with this Universal Energy and the healing energy it holds in every situation.

Here are a few other healing tools you can use Reiki with during your everyday life and some interesting ways to use them. Enjoy.

1. Healing/medicinal herbs or teas. Prior to using an herb to assist with healing during an illness, send Reiki to it for a minute or two, just as you would to bless food you were about to eat. Ask for the greatest good and send your intention/prayer.

Herbs can be seen as representing the Earth, so you may wish to offer a moment of thanks to the Earth for the healing plants she offers us. If you are having them in hot tea, you may also thank the water, the fire which heats it, the air which lifts the warm steam to your nostrils, making them feel so comforted and perhaps opening them when they are congested. Remember to thank Reiki as well, which is the life force energy which supports all of it and brings healing energy to you.

You may also find benefit in making herbal pouches or sachets to either wear or to place around your home. Their healing energy is amazing and they smell so divine! Rosemary, lavender, sage or rose are wonderful to bring a feeling of blessing, serenity and protection. Whatever you are using herbs for, offer them Reiki first and their benefits will increase.

2. Essential Oils. When you buy a bottle of essential oils, or when you are blending essential oils with a carrier oil, you can boost its beneficial properties by sending it Reiki for a couple minutes. Ask Reiki to work for the greatest good, as always.

A nice way to further use Reiki with essential oils is to apply a drop or two of an essential oil in a carrier oil, such as sesame, olive or jojoba oil, to your hands prior to doing your self Reiki treatment. You could also choose an oil that is good for anointing, such as frankincense, sandalwood or myrrh (use in a base oil, never alone), and touch a drop to each foot, hand and chakra point after your morning bath or shower, asking that each work that day in the purest possible Divine light.

3. Crystals and stones. The healing properties of any stone or crystal can be greatly magnified by sending Reiki to the stone. You can use Reiki with crystals and stones for a variety of purposes. Reiki can be used to cleanse the stone, to set an intention for the stone and charge it, you can even program a stone to release Reiki on its own, as needed, whenever it is for the greatest good.

Reiki grids using crystals have benefitted many, but very simple uses such as charging a crystal with Reiki and keeping it in your pocket, on your desk or nightstand is very useful as well. You can also write a concern on a piece of paper or draw a picture of something you are trying to work on, if you like. Then place one or more Reiki charged crystals on top of the paper, asking that they assist with the issue. I also always ask the assistance of my guides and Mother Mary. If you use this process, be prepared to let go of the issue after you set the intention and prayer. It may take time to resolve. But the process is very beneficial and can be useful for emotional issues, in particular.

Sending Reiki to medications and homeopathic remedies, or flower essences is also very beneficial. I find that herbs, essential oils, crystals and flower essences all have a very particular vibration all their own. I can feel their unique life force energies quite strongly and I enjoy honoring that with gratitude as part of the healing process. Tune in and notice the ways we are surrounded with life force! Honor it and embrace your ability to heal.

Reiki and Crystals

The ways to use crystals and gemstones in combination with Reiki may be as varied as the number of Reiki practitioners there are in the world today. Some prefer not to use crystals at all, either feeling no affinity with them or fearing that it will cause issues in their practice with those who do not believe that crystals are effective and find them a bit "woo-woo". There is no need to make a show of using crystals, if you choose to use them and don't want to cause a big stir.

You can use crystals simply by wearing one on your body, on a necklace or other piece of jewelry or by keeping them in your pocket. If you charge them with the purpose you intend, such as helping you stay grounded during the session, shielding or assisting you with the healing, they will be able to do their work from wherever they are.

Another option is to place the chosen crystals in the corners of the room, in inconspicuous places, or in other out of the way places around the room. Often, if these are placed in a decorative fashion and there is no fuss made over them, they simply look like any other part of the room decor. They will emit a calm and soothing energy that your client will likely not even be aware of.

Some practitioners place crystals underneath their Reiki table, in a crystal grid that is charged with assisting in the healing process, or with assisting in creating a calm and peaceful atmosphere for the healing process to take place. Grids can be created by simply following your own intuition in placing the crystals in position, listening to the vibration of each crystal as you place them. You will end up will a geometric pattern whose energy you can feel.

To properly and safely use crystals in Reiki, always cleanse your crystals before each session and again after each session. You can do this by allowing them to soak in a rinse of warm water with about a teaspoon of sea salt for 15-20 minutes. Other methods are to allow cold water to run over them for a few minutes or to run the crystal through a stream of smoke from burning sage or a smudge stick. If you have several clients in a day, you may need to use one of these faster methods during the day.

However, it is best to use the salt water soak at the end of the day and as often as possible between clients. Otherwise the crystals become bogged down with lots of people's energy and feel dense, full and heavy. Empaths and psychics can sometimes feel drained when around a crystal that needs to be cleansed.

Choose the crystals that you feel most drawn to for your Reiki room and for use on your own body or with clients. When using crystals to help align the chakras, it is often easiest to choose those that correspond to the color of the chakra you are working with. However, remember, Reiki always works to balance all the chakras.

Reiki Sleep Intentions

When you are in need of a good night's sleep but you have a problem weighing on your mind, racing around in thought circles through your head, don't just lie awake all night pondering a solution to the issue! Reiki can not only help you get a very good night's sleep, it can help you infuse your sleep with the intention to see a solution while you dream, so that you can drift off peacefully with the knowledge that the solution awaits you in your slumber.

To allow this process to happen, simply make yourself comfortable for sleep, with your pillow and blanket or whatever you like. Then allow your attention to rest on the problem you wish to find a solution to, without trying to force a solution to come. Draw the Reiki symbols, either mentally or in the air above you and ask that they carry into your mental state while you sleep and dream that night, intending that they help bring forth a solution to the problem you are focusing on. You may also wish to give Reiki to yourself on the head area, especially focusing on the back of the head and the crown area. Allow yourself to drift off into a peaceful and restful night's sleep.

Using this method, you will find that even problems that seem overwhelming will look very different to you by morning! You may find that a solution you never thought of is suddenly presented to you in a dream, or you may have a sudden understanding about the issue that brings new light to why the problem is occurring. No matter what, the way you see the problem will shift by morning and you will feel differently. And the lovely sleep you will get will help as well!

Remember to release any ideas about how you believe the problem needs to be solved before you do this! Your preconceived ideas about the problem and its possible solutions may be blocking you from seeing the solutions your subconscious mind already has available for you. Allow the Universe to bring them through by being open to all possibilities! Sweet dreams!

Chapter 7 – Allowing Reiki to Open Your Path

Allowing Reiki to Open Your Path

Fear can really get the better of us. It will close our hearts and our minds, making it impossible for us to trust the Divine or have faith in our own hearts. Being stuck in fear will cause us to keep choosing something that we know doesn't work simply because we are more afraid of taking a step in a new direction!

It is very vulnerable to step forward on a new path. It means opening your heart to the unknown and to possible hurt. Our systems may both tingle with excitement and bristle with warning at the thought of moving down a path we can't see.

Yet we all must walk in a new direction at some point. Life takes turns. Some are unforeseen and some you wouldn't miss for the world. Some you know are coming and you know they are necessary, but the change is so big you don't know where to go next or what to do. One thing is certain. If we try to stay in the same place, doing the same thing, the same way our whole lives, we limit our growth. Life is change, whatever that means for you.

Most of my life, I have been a person who took big leaps of faith, trusting my intuition and the Divine. I went down paths, literal and figurative, that some around me thought were risky or out of bounds. When I was in tune with this inner guidance, I had good life experiences, although they were sometimes bumpy. I learned a lot of valuable life lessons and as long as I trusted my inner guidance, I felt pretty good about where I was in life and where I was going.

Somewhere along the way, I slowly began to lose my confidence. I placed more and more value in the potential perspectives of others than in the flow of the Divine Spirit that had guided me. I never realized that the more I did this, the more power I gave them and the less I had to decide for myself what was right for me. I have been seeking to get my courage back, though I had no idea where to start.

When I start my day each day, I ask Reiki to flow to the day ahead. I do this when I travel somewhere as well, even if it's only to the store. I ask that Reiki flow to the car trip, all the cars on the road with me and to my destination. Essentially, I am always asking Reiki to flow ahead of me wherever it is I am about to go, for the greatest good. Ever since I began this practice, I have noticed that things go better when I do it. I feel better and things just seem to naturally fall into place more gracefully than when I neglect the practice.

I recently began to realize that **Reiki was helping me to regain my confidence** with taking my next steps forward on my life path. It seems like a natural progression that as I give myself Reiki every day and send Reiki ahead to all the situations I will be in, that Reiki would begin to ease my heart about taking the next steps in my life. I find that my old strength and courage is returning and I know that Reiki flows ahead of me on my path always.

I realized this at about the same time that I began working more with the archangels. After a long break from working with them, this was another area that I felt ready to return to. I feel Reiki guided me back. I now ask the angels and archangels to help guide me with peace in my heart every day, even when I don't know the next step. Their help combined with the Divine energy of Reiki has opened my heart and given me the freedom to keep moving to the next step and the next.

There is no way to explain how this works. It's not a step by step process. If you offer your heart and your path to be healed by the guidance of Reiki, it will open the way. **Allow the Divine and the Angels to guide you and heal you and trust the inner guidance** more than the old patterns and the fear that they may have established. You will likely find that your heart naturally begins to open more and you feel freer to allow this to happen. Keep using Reiki, trust and open yourself to the greatest and highest good.

Healing Isn't a Smooth Journey

There are a few misconceptions about the healing path that don't serve us very well. I would like to try and clear up the errors around these.

Being on a healing path doesn't meant that you will never get sick. It doesn't even mean that you will get well from whatever you have struggled with before you came to the healing journey. It often does mean that you recover as you begin to reveal the layers underneath the illness, but not always. Sometimes it simply means that you stop seeing yourself as a *"sick person"* or a victim and you develop a more functional way of living with what your body is like. That is healthier in and of itself. That feels better, even though the body still technically has an illness.

Mostly, being on a healing journey means that it is not a goal that you reach one day and then you are finished. **There is no finish line on a true healing journey.** You start to see that it is a process in which there are layers and the layers go deeper and deeper. That can sound frightening at the beginning, especially if you are in great physical and emotional pain. I understand. You want the pain to end—that is your goal. And that is OK.

But if you are to truly heal your pain, you must heal each of the layers that created it. That is a learning and growing process, a shedding of the things that do not work. As you do this, tools will present themselves to you which help you along the path. They help you to continue shedding layers and growing, doing the work of healing. As you work through the layers, revealing new insights about yourself, you will start to see that there is a wonderful jewel inside you. **You will see that the process of healing has value as a journey, as a way of being, not as a goal.** And at some point, you will begin to value yourself and wherever you are in your life, in each moment—even the unpleasant ones. That is pretty powerful.

The healing path is not an easy one to walk. This is another misconception I very often see, especially when people comment on one of my articles or speak to me in person. Even loved ones have mistaken this. I have often said that finding the healing path changed my life. That is very true. In fact, I don't doubt that it saved my life. I have a very positive and appreciative way of viewing life and I am much healthier than I used to be. But that didn't happen immediately. It was, and still is, a path. There are many course corrections; days where I have to repeatedly remind myself of the direction I want to be heading. And especially in those first months and years, it was very difficult as I worked through the density of the unhealed layers of myself. It took determination to get through it. The alternative of continuing to live unhealed and in pain was worse. Though I am happier and healthier, that doesn't mean I never feel sad, angry or fearful and it doesn't mean I never get sick or have pain. I am still human. The way I handle these things has changed.

The healing journey does not mean that everything comes easily or that each day is joyous and carefree. Life still goes on. Some days will be challenging. You will still feel emotions—even unpleasant ones. That's normal. Some days you will see old patterns peek to the surface, especially in the beginning or when you expose yourself to situations that trigger those. As you learn, you will grow, but you will never be perfect. **Perfection doesn't exist.** Even Jesus needed someone to help him as he carried his cross. This life is very challenging at times! It takes effort to continue learning your way through being a human! Remember to be gentle and supportive with yourself. **Ask for help when you need it and allow yourself to be human, imperfect and loved.**

The Spiritual Path after Reiki

Many people have a lot of expectations about themselves and what will happen with their lives after they take a Reiki class and become attuned to Reiki. Some of these expectations are not realistic or healthy and lead to them holding themselves to extremely high levels of perfectionism. Reiki training does not make you or your life perfect. It teaches you a method of energy healing. For many, it is also an opening or an expansion of their spiritual path.

Being on a spiritual path or intensifying your spiritual seeking can become a very trying time for many. This opens the doors to all the issues that need to be examined and healed and in some people it does so quite suddenly. This can be shocking and overwhelming at the beginning. Walking a spiritual path requires being truthful with ourselves over and over, accepting our reality as it is without slipping into denial or a reactive state. This is a practice, every single day. It requires compassion, with ourselves, others and life itself.

It can help if you approach all of life as an opportunity to learn, with each person you meet and each situation as a potential lesson. When you seek to find what you can learn and grow from in each encounter, then everyday events have purpose. It is possible to acknowledge that even difficult events in life have meaning. Looking back over your life, you can likely see that each event, difficult or otherwise, brought you to the place and the possibilities you have now. Without any one of those, you would change important features of your life, perhaps not meeting the loved ones or the gaining the knowledge that you have now. Each event serves you and the world in some way that you aren't always able to see in the moment. Some events allow for us to be in the right place to assist others in their growth or healing, even if we don't know it.

There is no need to beat yourself up if you are not doing some particular thing or other that you envisioned you would be doing once you were attuned to Reiki or once you started on your spiritual path. There is no specific "place" or destination you are meant to achieve. There is no state of mind you are meant to maintain. You are still human after learning Reiki. Be kind to yourself. Relax and enjoy life.

The best thing you can do to assist yourself as a healer and to help yourself on your path of spiritual growth is to keep it simple. There is no need to complicate matters. The following list may be oversimplifying things and each person is an individual, but adjust it to yourself and go with the flow.

1.   **Practice Reiki. Especially on yourself.** Even if you aren't practicing on anyone else, practicing on yourself keeps you in tune with the energy and helps keep you in balance mentally, emotionally, spiritually and physically.

2.   **Meditate.** This doesn't have to be complicated either! Just notice your breathing for at least a few minutes a day. No need to get in any particular position, just be comfortable. No need for visualizing anything or for having a blank mind. Guide your mind back to your breath when it wanders away. That's exactly the process! Even 3-5 minutes is beneficial, but do it for whatever length of time works for you.

3.   **Learn to trust your inner voice.** When you have a strong intuition, practice acting on it. Write these instances down to keep track of what happens. Also record those times when your intuition is more subtle or when you are afraid to act on it. Notice the results of that as well.

4.   **Don't get caught up in your intuition or your healing abilities.** We all have these skills. You are simply opening yourself to them and making use of them. You are not doing yourself a service if you feel "gifted" or superior.

5.   **Be loving with yourself and others.** Remember to play, laugh and love! That is key to everything else. Relax. This is what the 5 precepts are teaching you. Spend 5 minutes or so thinking of them each day to tune in to these reminders of peaceful living.

Try to accept life as it comes. Notice that the "good" comes in and flows out and so does the "bad". In the end they all serve a purpose somehow. They can each cause pain if we get overly caught up in them, judging them, trying to make them go away or trying to cling to them. Let life be like a flowing river that you observe and participate in lovingly.

Reiki and Christianity

I often hear of Christians who are afraid to accept or practice Reiki because they feel it is going against Christianity and the teachings of Christ. It is not necessary for either the practitioner or the recipient to follow a particular belief system, or any belief system at all in order for Reiki to work. Reiki is not dependent on religion. I would not tell someone what to believe. But I would like to show various ways in which Reiki is in alignment with what Jesus taught.

1.   **Jesus was a healer.** This is not denied by any Christian that I know. There are a great many instances of Jesus healing people in body, mind, and spirit.

2.   **Jesus taught others to heal.** He taught all of his disciples how to heal, and often encouraged their efforts and corrected them so they might heal more effectively.

3.   **Jesus said that all who learned from him would do the things He did and more.** In the book of John, Jesus said that others would be able to do everything He did. They only needed to believe they could. "Do not fear, only believe," He told the grieving father whose little girl had apparently died.

4.   **Jesus was compassionate.** Jesus taught love and compassion above all. He asked that we all love and help our "neighbors", which He described as anyone and everyone. It seems He wanted all to receive healing and love. He healed

His followers as well as those who were of other cultures and religions. Healing was for all.

5.   **The early Christians seemed to realize that healing was teachable to all.** The parts of the New Testament that take place after the death of Jesus have many instances of healing done by Christ's followers. Paul and Peter, in particular, were frequent healers and taught other followers that they should do the same.

6.   **The Reiki principles embody the teachings of Jesus.** When we say the "Just for today..." principles and follow our path of spiritual seeking, we are in alignment with what Jesus taught. We do not have to be Christians to practice calmness, compassion, kindness and respect for self and others. These principles are inherent in all forms of spiritual practice and in coping well with life.

The primary purpose of following Jesus is to learn His teachings and then embrace and embody them. Healing is doing just that. To receive healing in modern times is no different than it was for those receiving healing from Jesus or his disciples. The healing Reiki energy comes from Source. This healing energy flowing from the Divine is mentioned all throughout the Bible (Old and New Testament). Jesus was a teacher in how to use and direct this flow of energy for the greatest and highest good.

What is "Spiritual Healing"?

When I first began writing for Reiki Rays, I wrote Reiki and Christianity. My intention was to address a few of the many spiritual questions surrounding Reiki, particularly as I had seen them arise in relation to Christians. Since that time, I have experienced more with Reiki, with the online community through writing about Reiki and with speaking to the public about Reiki. I have heard many questions, fears and misunderstandings in relation to Reiki and other types of energy healing, so I'd like to write another article that goes a little deeper and explores a little more broadly on the subject.

Many have heard that Reiki is energy healing or spiritual healing, but what does that mean exactly? It can sound a little vague and that can leave lots of room for misinterpretation.

Everything in the Universe is energy. This is not only a concept that has been explored in all major religions and spiritual traditions, but has been the acknowledged basis for most ancient healing traditions. Modern science has since caught up to this fact and is expanding its understanding of it and the way in which it studies it and speaks about it.

We all have various types of energy that courses through our bodies and around our bodies all the time. We could refer to the main energy that keeps us alive as *"life force energy"*. This is only one way to think of it, but it is a fairly common term to hear among energy healers. This can also be called prana, qi, chi, or ki. Another term is spirit. This is why Reiki is often referred to as spiritual healing. Not because it is related to teaching or counseling us about spirituality or altering the course of our spiritual path.

There is nothing particularly mysterious about this energy, no more so than other types of energy. The thing that makes it seem so is that most people don't see it, can't sense it and aren't aware of it. There are hundreds, perhaps thousands of types of energy that we are not aware of on a daily basis, and yet they are there and we constantly make use of them and interact with them. Sunlight alone has many different kinds of energy and we have only been able to detect some of them in recent centuries. Consider the normal use that we get from microwave energy and x-ray energy every day in the modern world, or from the electricity that powers our appliances and the Wi-Fi signal which allows the connection of our internet. We take these energies for granted all day long, and yet we had no idea they existed 150 years ago.

Energy is everywhere and we are literally alive because of it. Our brains and our hearts function because of energy signals. The cells of our bodies and the neurons of our brains interact with each other because of energy. We interact with others and the world because of energy signals that we give and receive. This is not religion or new age woo-woo fluffy nonsense. This is factual science which can be looked up anywhere. This is the basis of energy medicine. The approaches may be different, but the basis is in energy and keeping it balanced and flowing in a healthy manner.

Many see the life force energy as being what connects us to our Higher Power, or God. Reiki is considered Universal Energy, which could be seen as the source of all life force energy, where all energy flows from. That depends upon your view. However, no matter what your views, the energy remains. Your health and well-being are influenced by how your energy flows in your body. That is not affected by your religious affiliation or lack thereof, nor by the Reiki practitioner's views or affiliations.

Though many religious and spiritual traditions have recognized this energy, there is no religious tie to Reiki. Reiki is not anti-religion. It is simply energy based and makes no particular affiliation. Just as a doctor, massage therapist or acupuncturist may have their own spiritual views and beliefs and it has no influence on the work they do, a practitioner's individual beliefs are not the basis of the work we do in Reiki. The work is energy based. It works directly with the Universal Source of all life force, for the greatest and highest good, to bring a greater balance to your energy field, but makes no particular judgement about how to see that or what to call it. All of that is very human based and Universal Energy doesn't concern itself with that. It simply is.

If your beliefs are that you are doing spiritual harm to yourself by receiving Reiki, then you should not receive it. Receive some other type of healing. The fear that you carry will create blockage in your energy and that alone will cause problems. Fear is energy. It sends many signals to your body, mind and the world around you, which are responded to. Examine those fears first if Reiki interests you. Another option is to find a Reiki practitioner who has similar beliefs to your own. There are Reiki practitioners of nearly every religion or spiritual tradition. Some seeking should easily lead you to the right match for you.

Bless and De-stress

The primary thing that causes illness is what we refer to as stress. This is a blanket term that includes most anything that creates resistance to balance and happiness. That can include trauma, unreleased negative emotions, physical injury, unhealthy diet, negative environment and other factors. When our minds or bodies are in a state of stress much of the time and are not able to release it, we tend to become ill or stay ill.

If we want to create an environment that is conducive to health and healing, we have to reverse the stress factor. When the body is not in a state of stress, it naturally works to begin any needed healing and repair. Reiki is one thing that helps the body do this beautifully. It creates a deep state of relaxation, which allows the body's own healing response to activate. When used as a hands on treatment, as it often is when done in person, Reiki also provides the benefit of touch, which is so critical to our sense of well-being. While some people prefer not to be touched, or to have very limited touch, humans generally require a certain amount of touch in order to be at their healthiest.

When we want to make a difference in our health by reversing stress, the most effective way to do that is to begin **changing the way we deal with life** on a day to day and minute to minute basis. Most of us are overwhelmed at the thought of suddenly changing our lives, and it doesn't need to be very drastic. Baby steps are the best way to make most changes.

It took a long time to build the attitudes and defenses you have today and they are there because you need them for some reason. Trying to tear them all down at one time, before you are ready can do more harm than good, and will only create new stress. Taking small steps, making the changes that feel comfortable to you right now will create growth at a pace that makes sense for you.

One small thing you can begin to do that will go a long way toward shifting your attitude and reducing your stress is to **reduce criticism and replace it with gratitude**. This doesn't take a lot of time or require you to make any changes to the structure of your life, but it can take a lot of mental effort to implement if you have become stuck in self-criticism. Self-criticism often becomes criticism of others and of life in general. All of these things build toxic emotions all through the day, every day, leading to illness and pain. These thought habits are also destructive to the possibility of healthy relationships.

You can begin the process of replacing self-criticism with gratitude by practicing awareness throughout the day. This is also known as mindfulness. Set the intention each morning when you wake up that you will notice your thoughts as you go through the day. When you notice a critical thought, especially if it is directed at yourself, stop, take a deep breath or two and notice what you are feeling and thinking. Do not place any judgment on the feelings and thoughts, even if it is tempting to do so. The point is to observe them and become aware of what they are. You are learning about yourself.

You may notice that the feelings are painful or uncomfortable. Offer compassion to yourself, maybe by placing your hand over your heart or by giving yourself Reiki for a moment. Even a simple kind thought, such as *"It's OK. I accept you,"* can be very helpful. Speak to yourself as kindly as you would speak to a friend or a child who is hurting.

It is also helpful to set the **intention each morning that you will find one thing to have gratitude for** that day that you had not thought to be grateful for before. Maybe it can be something that has to do with the thing or person you are having the most difficulty not criticizing. See it as a means of blessing the situation rather than stressing over it. In fact, you will find that the more situations and people you can find to send a blessing to throughout your day, the more fulfilled and blessed you will feel. Your stress will naturally decrease, even if you do little else and your life will begin to shift.

Chapter 8 – Reiki History

The Real (?) Story of Reiki - Part 1 - Usui and Hayashi

What is the true story of Reiki? Should we base our practice strictly on tradition? If so, what is that tradition? There are so many inconsistent stories of the history of Reiki, how can we know? Is change OK? I love learning and when I first began learning about the Reiki story, the inconsistencies baffled me.

Mikao Usui

When I later discovered William Rand's research in Reiki, The Healing Touch, I was impressed. He has dedicated a great deal of time to learning more about Mikao Usui and the history of Reiki. He has travelled to Japan and spoken to members of the Gakkai, the organization founded by Usui, and has received training from members of the Gakkai as part of his quest to understand the Japanese perspective better. In addition to researching material to help him understand the history better, he visited many sites relating to Mikao Usui's life and death, gathering information that could be verified.

According to Rand, Usui, the founder of Reiki, was a student at a Tendai Buddhist school from the age of four. He studied qigong and later he studied medicine, psychology, religion (particularly Christianity and Buddhism), history, divination and the art of studying and reading faces. He was dedicated to helping others, often choosing jobs that allowed him to do that, and was a lifelong spiritual aspirant. In 1922, he was having major personal and business difficulties and chose to go spend a 21 day training retreat on Mt. Kurama near where he had gone to school as a boy. His hopes were that the time in meditation would bring a solution to his problems to mind. He doesn't seem to have been seeking to discover a method of healing at all! During the retreat, he received Reiki. He became excited and ran to tell others, stubbing his toe as he ran. He put his hand over the toe, as anyone would, and felt the Reiki energy flooding into the injury automatically. It quickly relieved the pain, making him realize that he had not only received the light of Reiki, but now had the gift of healing as well.

Usui continued to develop the practice of Reiki, using the skills he had from his previous studies and through Reiki practicing on family. He eventually decided to share Reiki with others by practicing it in his clinics and through his healing society, called the Usui Reiki Ryoho Gakkai, through which he taught others how to use Reiki.

Eventually, Usui encouraged one of his students, a medical doctor and former Naval officer named Chujiro Hayashi, to open a Reiki clinic as well. Hayashi opened his clinic and school shortly before Usui died. Soon after Usui passed due to a stroke in 1926, Hayashi left the Gakkai to run his school and clinic on his own. He adapted his methods a bit, according to his style as a doctor and what proved to work best with patients over time, developing his own training manual based upon careful records of which hand positions were most effective. He also began treating patients on a treatment table, which Usui had apparently not been doing. (Some sources say Usui treated on a mat on the floor; Rand say he used a chair.) He altered training and attunement methods as well, making attunements more effective and shortening training schedules when traveling to students. Hayahsi trained Mrs. Takata, who brought Reiki to the West. Hayahsi died after committing ritual suicide when he refused to give information to the Japanese regarding military targets that he may have seen in Hawaii during his visit to establish Mrs. Takata as a Reiki Master. He died an honorable death in 1940.

The Real (?) Story of Reiki - Part 2 - Mrs. Takata

Mrs. Takata brought Reiki to the West from Japan at a very difficult time. There were enormous tensions between the United States and Japan when she returned to Hawaii, just years prior to the attack on Pearl Harbor. All things from Japan were feared and hated during the years prior to Pearl Harbor, and especially so afterwards. Discussing Reiki must have been a huge challenge, requiring bravery. After the attack, she was completely isolated in the West as a Reiki Master. Her own Master, Chujiro Hayashi, was dead and the Gakai in Japan had become a secret society in order to avoid regulation or shut down. She had learned Reiki as a widowed mother who encountered Reiki in Japan during a visit to her parents. She had been ill and sought Reiki to avoid surgery for a multitude of health issues. She was amazed and stayed on to learn, working at Hayashi's for clinic to pay for her training as she learned.

Mrs. Takata changed a number of things about the way she taught Reiki. She did not use a manual, as Hayashi did, but taught a strictly oral form of the classes. She would not even allow students to tape record the classes or write down the symbols or take notes during class. Everything had to be done orally. Rand's research shows that this was not how Usui or

Hayashi taught and that Takata received a manual when she learned, so we can only speculate why she chose to do this. She also standardized the hand positions so that all treatments were the same and she did not use techniques that were used in the Japanese tradition. Takata also swore her students to a very strict code about what to charge for training new Reiki students and Masters, such as the fee of $10,000 for Reiki Master training, which is almost never used today.

One thing Mrs. Takata changed a great deal was the story of Reiki. Most say she adjusted her story according to the group she was speaking to and seldom told the Reiki story the same way twice. Most say it wasn't that she was lying, it was that she had a method of telling a story in a very Hawaiian style, which calls for embellishment and understanding the dynamics of the group you are speaking to. Or maybe she simply felt isolated and felt a need to create a wonder and respect for Reiki in her own way. We are ever in her debt for bringing Reiki to the West and around the world in such a difficult time, forging forward and protecting it in whatever way she could.

Reiki has evolved tremendously since Mrs. Takata died in 1980 and continues to spread. Some swear by "tradition" and don't want to see a change at all. Others are eager to embrace rapid change. As you can see, change has been part of Reiki from the beginning. Careful, constructive change can only benefit. Rigidly clinging to old ways that don't make sense any more or that weren't based in fact, doesn't serve us or our clients.

My Path to Reiki

The road that led me to Reiki has had many twists and turns. I have been empathic and able to sense energy as long as I can remember. It wasn't something I could control; it just happened. I learned not to talk about this.

I was able to communicate with animals. I could tell what their fears and pains were, as well as what made them happy. As I got older, I instinctively learned that reaching out to animals through touch or communication often calmed them and helped them with problems they had. I had an intense need to be around animals and to be outside.

As an adult, I feared that being my true self might cause problems for me, so I suppressed my truth even further. Doing this caused an imbalance in my energy. I could feel that things were maladjusted in me, but I was more fearful of the punishment from others than I was for my own well-being. This made me quite sick. I had seizures so many times a day that I could no longer form new memories. I often didn't recall what I had done moments before. The past, present and future were jumbled up in my head, as if there were no difference between them. I was in a great deal of physical and psychic pain.

I had a near death experience that changed my outlook on life. I returned to the physical body with a deeper knowledge of Spirit and why I was here. It took me many more years to understand that I needed to release all previous ideas of what life had in store for me. I knew I needed to heal, and I got serious about that.

When I was asked not to come back to a church I had been attending, my world fell apart. I began searching for deeper answers by trying to understand the human history of religion. I read as many different religious and spiritual books as I could find. In the end, I saw that they all have essentially the same message as my Bible does. Love, be compassionate, do not judge, help and heal as many as you can, be at peace, do not fear. I began by healing myself. I practiced these principles of love and healing and I sent love and healing to any that needed it.

I developed a longing to help that I felt as a throbbing, burning in my sacral charka. I felt that somehow I was called to spread healing to many, to help. I had no idea how to do it. Through a website about Ho'oponopono, I heard of energy healing and my life changed. This began a new path of studying all I could find about energy medicine.

As soon as I learned what Reiki was, I knew I wanted to be attuned. I sought out a Reiki session and was immediately convinced that this was what I had searched for. The ache in my lower belly eased as I sought a Reiki Master. I felt I had found myself and my true purpose. Being attuned to Reiki was the next step in my self-healing. I can now see that everything that led me to Reiki happened in Divine Order. Reiki was seeking me all along.

About the Author

Angie Webster is a freelance writer, Reiki Master Teacher and meditation teacher. Angie's primary focus in her Reiki practice is empowering women with chronic pain conditions, neurological conditions or anxiety. She offers guided meditation and shamanic Reiki as part of her practice, where appropriate. Angie is the author of **Infinite Reiki, Infinite Healing: How Energy Medicine Healed my Life and What It Can do for Yours.** *Reiki and a healthy lifestyle contributed to her healing after a 20 year struggle with neurological and chronic pain issues. She comes out the other side with a new perspective on life and now seeks to empower others, guiding them back to their own innate healing abilities.*

You can follow her at:

http://naturalholisticlife.wordpress.com/,https://www.facebook.com /HolisticSpirituality, http://www.serenityenergyhealing.com/

Appendix 1 – Reiki Hand Positions for Self Healing

Reiki Hand Positions
for self-treatment
Reiki Rays © 2013
http://reikirays.com

Made in the USA
Monee, IL
11 October 2022

15679354R00155